"In a time of crisis, when so many young people have abandoned the Church, Brandon Vogt stands out among his generation as one who boldly affirms the truth, goodness, and beauty of the Catholic faith. As this book demonstrates, he is bright, articulate, kind, and passionate. He's one of the radiant lights of the New Evangelization."

Most Rev. Robert Barron
Auxiliary Bishop of Los Angeles

"Brandon Vogt has written an insightful case for the Catholic faith. His treatment on how beauty confirms the truth of Catholicism is one of the best I've ever read."

Trent Horn
An apologist at Catholic Answers and author of *Answering Atheism*

"*Why I Am Catholic* proposes a most winning account, one that will tug most any reader toward fondness for the faith."

Christopher Kaczor
America

"Like all of Brandon Vogt's writing, his compelling new book is accessible, inviting, practical, inspirational, and, in the deepest sense, true."

Rev. James Martin, S.J.
Author of *The Jesuit Guide to (Almost) Everything*

"For years, I've longed for a book that I could recommend to parents whose children have left the Church or to people who have lost their faith. This is that book. Brandon Vogt makes the case for Catholicism with remarkable clarity and charity. Along the way, he handles common objections to Catholicism with answers that touch both mind and heart. If you know someone struggling with belief—or if you yourself have questions or doubts—then do yourself a favor: buy this book, read it, and then share it with others."

Brant Pitre
Catholic theologian, speaker, and author of *The Case for Jesus*

"Superb. Concise, readable, and substantive. Amazing."

Tom Neal
Professor of spiritual theology and director of lay programs
Notre Dame Seminary

"Brandon Vogt is one of my spiritual mentors, role models, and prayer warriors. I love *Why I Am Catholic*, in which Brandon provides guidance to a world in need of compassion and reason."

Lisa M. Hendey
Founder of *CatholicMom.com* and author of *The Grace of Yes*

"I wish I'd read this book back when I was an atheist—I would have become Catholic much sooner! Brandon Vogt makes clear, reasonable arguments that will resonate with people from any faith background."

Jennifer Fulwiler
Catholic radio host and author of *Something Other Than God*

"This book is clear, concise, and persuasive all in the same breath. Seeing the Church's truth, goodness, and beauty so effortlessly spelled out without getting too technical is truly masterful."

Matthew Sewell
National Catholic Register

Why I Am Catholic

(AND YOU SHOULD BE TOO)

BRANDON VOGT

AVE MARIA PRESS AVE Notre Dame, Indiana

Founded in 1865, Ave Maria Press is a ministry of the United States Province of Holy Cross.

www.avemariapress.com

Hardcover: ISBN-13 978-1-59471-767-3

Paperback: ISBN-13 978-1-59471-903-5

E-book: ISBN-13 978-1-59471-768-0

Cover image © Greg Dale / Exactostock-1701.

Cover and text design by Andy Wagoner.

Printed and bound in the United States of America.

Library of Congress Cataloging-in-Publication Data

Names: Vogt, Brandon, author.
Title: Why I am Catholic (and you should be too) / Brandon Vogt.
Description: Notre Dame : Ave Maria Press, 2017. | Includes bibliographical references.
Identifiers: LCCN 2017010887 (print) | LCCN 2017027426 (ebook) | ISBN 9781594717680 (ebook) | ISBN 9781594717673 (hardcover)
Subjects: LCSH: Catholic Church--Apologetic works.
Classification: LCC BX1752 (ebook) | LCC BX1752 .V64 2017 (print) | DDC 282--dc23
LC record available at https://lccn.loc.gov/2017010887

To Bishop Robert Barron
I'm grateful for your influence;
this book is filled with it.
I'm grateful for your friendship and
fatherhood; they've marked my life.
And I'm grateful for you; you're a
main reason why I am Catholic.

It is impossible to be just to the Catholic Church. The moment a man ceases to pull against it he feels a tug towards it. The moment he ceases to shout it down he begins to listen to it with pleasure. The moment he tries to be fair to it he begins to be fond of it.

—G. K. Chesterton, Catholic convert

Contents

Preface to the Paperback Edition

Recently, while in Rome for some meetings, I had a chance to visit a few of the city's popular plazas and squares with some friends and a video camera. Our goal was to interview young people at random and discover what they thought about God, religion, and the Catholic Church.

We asked simple questions like "What is God?", "Can you name any saints?", and "What's the most important thing Jesus ever did?" Most of the answers were confused or disappointing. "I don't know" was the most common reply.

But one question generated lots of responses. We asked young people, "What's the best and worst thing the Catholic Church has ever done?" Only a few people could think of anything *good* associated with the Catholic Church. Some gestured to the beautiful artwork and churches that surrounded us in Rome. One young woman acknowledged that the Catholic Church greatly helped the poor ("but a long time ago," she added, "not so much now").

Most revealing were the answers to the second part of that question, about the *worst* thing the Church has ever done. Several people mentioned the Inquisition or the

Crusades. However, by far the most common answer was "the sexual abuse of kids." Nearly everyone mentioned it. Most strikingly, one person reflected for a moment, then said, "It's tough for me to answer that question because I honestly don't know which is worse: killing people or raping young kids."

Between the publication of the first edition of this book in October 2017 and these street interviews a year later, the Church was rocked by new revelations of sexual abuse and cover-up. Many American Catholics thought that after the bombshell abuse revelations in 2002, the worst was behind them. They were wrong.

An avalanche of new scandals tumbled into the news, from the account of a high-ranking Cardinal accused of abusing young men to grand jury reports chronicling decades of abuse against hundreds of victims in one state alone. The stories are harrowing. Even the few I read made me nauseated and enraged, especially as a father of six young children. And though the majority of these cases occurred in the pastmostly during the fifties, sixties, and seventiesit's clear that many Church leaders still don't recognize the gravity of these abuses.

Those initial reports have since been followed by near-daily revelations of sexual impropriety at seminaries, bishops shuffling abusive priests between parishes, and Church leaders not only failing to address the problems but also actively participating in them.

Without question, the revelations of the summer of 2018 have established the last few decades as one of the darkest periods in American Church history. And that has caused many Catholics to understandably wonder why they should remain Catholic. How can I remain associated with such a corrupt institution? How can I keep my children in Catholic parishes and schools if the Church seems incapable of protecting them from sexual abuse? These are questions I've asked myself.

At the same time, people outside the Church who are considering becoming Catholic must wonder, Why should I *become* Catholic in light of all this sickening news? Wouldn't life be easier in some other church or religion? Those are good questions, too.

So, in a book titled *Why I Am Catholic*, I can't avoid the elephant in the room, the most obvious reason *not* to be Catholic: the sexual abuse crisis. In response, I've written this preface to answer why I, a Millennial Catholic, young husband, and father, remain Catholic despite these horrific cases of abuse and cover-up.

The main answer is that I'm Catholic because of Jesus, not because of the leaders of the Church. As you'll see in this book, the principal reason to become Catholic is because you're convinced Catholicism is true and you believe what the Church teaches about faith, morals, and its own identity. I'm convinced Catholicism is true because of Jesus. I believe the Church wasn't just started by a group of bumbling bureaucrats but by Jesus himself, God in the flesh.

It's Jesus I'm drawn to, Jesus I'm committed to, and Jesus I trust. It's true that Catholics are often drawn to the faith by charismatic leaders, warm parish communities, or impressive schools. There's nothing wrong with those entry points, as long as we remember that our faith is not ultimately rooted in those things and isn't compromised when they fail.

As a Catholic, my faith is in Jesus Christ, not his followers. When sin and evil swirl through the Church, I keep my eyes fixed on that reliable center, that untainted source of the Church's authority and attraction: Jesus.

My second answer is that I know that the sexual abuse crisis is not indicative of the entire Church. The percentage of priests and bishops complicit in these crimes is relatively low (smaller, in fact, than in many other religions). The vast majority of priests and bishops are good, holy men who are just as disgusted as the laity about this abuse. Some of my closest friends are priests and they're among the most selfless, virtuous people I know.

One reason there's so much outrage over sexually abusive priests is because most people know, intuitively, that priests are supposed to be moral exemplars. I'm convinced that most still are, and it's a reason I remain close to them.

My third and final answer is that I remain Catholic because I want to be part of the solution. The Church is not just an institution but also a family, and when your family faces a crisis, you don't flee—you stay and help. When we experience evil or terror, our natural reaction is to run. That's understandable; we're scared and scandalized.

But for Catholics, the Church is our family and home; and when evil threatens your family or home, you don't give up and run away. You batten down the hatches. You plant your feet. You resolve, "This is *my* home, and I will *not* let evil destroy it."

Or, to switch metaphors, when a family member has cancer, you don't just give up on them and leave. You move closer to them. You resolve to stay by their side and help battle the cancer. You give all you can offer.

That's what the Catholic Church needs now. In times of crisis—and there have been many such crises throughout the Church's history (and indeed there will be more)—the Church summons new heroes who are committed to holiness and driven to uproot whatever sin and evil have infected the spiritual family.

So, scandals don't push me away from the Church, just as a relative's cancer diagnosis doesn't push me away from her. In both cases, the evil demands a heroic resolve to stay and fight, to be part of the solution, especially on behalf of the victims.

I want to be very clear: these sexual abuse cases are horrific. There's no downplaying them or justifying them or explaining them away. They're egregious and scandalizing. But Catholicism doesn't fall when its members fail. I'm Catholic not because Church leaders are perfect, but because the Church channels to me the love and forgiveness of Jesus in unparalleled ways: his body and blood in the Eucharist, his forgiveness in Confession.

Life may seem easier outside the Church. But these divine treasures are only found within, and they carry Catholics through even the darkest of times.

Brandon Vogt

The Only Rebellion Left

Anything but Catholic.

Spirituality, great. Religion, fine. Attending church, maybe.

But why in the world would anyone become Catholic today? Isn't Catholicism a backward, intolerant, bigoted religion? Isn't it run by pedophile priests and full of scandals? Doesn't it degrade women and LGBT people and obsess about sex? Isn't it plagued by pointless rules that stifle real faith?

I was not raised Catholic. Some of my friends must have been Catholic growing up, but I never knew it. I grew up in a Presbyterian church, which provided a warm community and great formation. Yet like many young people, the life of faith never took root in me. This was almost certainly my fault, not the church's.

As a teenager, I probably would have identified as "spiritual but not religious." But then in college at Florida State, while studying mechanical engineering, I fell in with a Methodist group on campus, which dramatically affected my faith. I found a deep, vibrant community that welcomed me in. They weren't afraid of hard questions, and they exposed me to the fascinating world of the Bible. I started praying on my own and began devouring books about God and faith and philosophy.

But then, as a twenty-year-old senior with a budding faith, and on the cusp of graduating, getting married, and starting a new engineering job, I did something few people could fathom, something that didn't fit with all those other sensible decisions: I became Catholic.

To say friends and family were surprised would be a vast understatement. Most were profoundly confused, and remain so. Though I've discussed it often, trying to explain what led me into the Church, it's still hard for people to understand how a young man with an apparently well-functioning brain would not only look favorably on an institution such as the Catholic Church but also actually choose to join it.

It's been eight years since I chose to become Catholic. Interestingly, I've noted how different the reaction I usually get compares to the reactions that converts to other religions often receive. Admit you're exploring Buddhism and you're greeted with wonder and encouragement. Reveal that you've become Jewish or Muslim and you're treated with hushed reverence. Say you're dedicated to meditation or the power of positive thinking and the "Good for you" comments will stream out as if you lost sixty pounds. Heck, share that you've just been baptized at a local nondenominational church and people will congratulate you on such a wonderful milestone.

But admit you're becoming Catholic? Crickets and confusion.

Choosing to be Catholic is provocative. It's countercultural. It's literally the opposite direction our culture is going. The Pew Research Center completed a massive, national religious study, surveying more than thirty thousand Americans, which found that exactly half (50 percent) of millennials who were raised Catholic no longer call themselves Catholic today. That's massive attrition. Half of young Catholics have already left the Church (with more likely following in the future). That explains why "former Catholic" continues to be one of America's largest religious groups.

The study also found that roughly 80 percent of people who left the Catholic Church have left before age twenty-three. These aren't lifelong Catholics who stay on the fence for decades before drifting away. They're young people, people in high school or college, or young adults— people the same age I was when I chose to *become* Catholic.

Perhaps most telling, the Pew study revealed something called the "loss-gain ratio." This is the ratio of people who *leave* a particular religious tradition divided by the people who *join* (excluding births and deaths). Ideally, you want your loss-gain ratio to be less than one, meaning your religion is losing fewer people than you're gaining. Unfortunately, in the latest survey, no Christian group had a loss-gain ratio less than one. In other words, every Christian tradition is losing more people than it's gaining. But do you know which religious group owned the worst loss-gain ratio of all? Catholicism.

The Catholic Church's loss-gain ratio was a staggering 6.45. That means for every one person walking in the front door of the Catholic Church, more than six leave through the back door. That's a worse ratio than Baptists, Evangelicals, Methodists, Mormons, Muslims, Jews, and Hindus—even worse than atheists and agnostics!

The Catholic Church is hemorrhaging people, *especially* young people. So *why* be Catholic? Surely anything else would be better, maybe some other form of Christianity, or even a mystical Eastern faith, or perhaps some do-it-yourself spirituality.

But why Catholic? I wrote this book to answer that question.

I'm not part of the 50 percent of millennials who left the Church. I'm not one of the 6.45 who continually stream out the back door. I'm the one who joined. I'm the one who deliberately chose Catholicism, who carefully studied and wrestled with its claims, who prayed, read, thought, and discussed and came out the other end a Catholic.

I'll admit it's a weird decision. It goes against the grain. It's radical. It is, in a word, rebellious.

But that's precisely what makes it worth considering (and, dare I say, exciting). It's easy to swim downstream, to accept the status quo. What's hard is to be a rebel, to look with fresh eyes on something most people reject and say, "What if they're mistaken? What if 'anything but Catholic' should perhaps be 'what else *but* Catholic'?"

These same questions struck G. K. Chesterton. He was one of the most popular and prolific English journalists of the early twentieth century, writing more than a hundred books and more than five thousand essays, and lecturing all over the globe. But in 1922, he stunned the world by announcing his conversion to the Catholic Church. Friends and family were just as confused as mine were almost a century later. They thought this normally straight mind had gone horribly off the rails, asking him accusingly, "*Why* would you become Catholic?"

Chesterton replied, as was his wont, with an essay. He titled it, plainly, "Why I Am a Catholic," and he began it by saying, "The difficulty of explaining why I am a Catholic is that there are ten thousand reasons all amounting to one reason: that Catholicism is true."[1]

That's a great answer, and it's mine too. It's the main reason to accept any belief, philosophy, or worldview. Whether we're talking about Christianity, evolution, democracy, or atheism, what matters most is that fundamental question: Is it true? Sure, a particular view may make us feel better. Perhaps it puts us in good company or is rooted in our family's heritage. But ultimately, the best reason to accept any belief is because it's true. Like Socrates, we should assess the evidence and follow it wherever it leads, even to conclusions that are unpopular or uncomfortable. That's what truth demands.

Of course, there are other good reasons to believe something. If a belief is true, it's almost always good and beautiful too. There's a harmony among these three qualities, what philosophers call the transcendentals. For example, look at science. Even atheist scientists such as Stephen

Hawking and Richard Dawkins speak about the elegance
and majesty of the universe. The remarkable order we see
in nature strikes us not only because it's true, because it
matches our equations, but also because it's surprisingly
beautiful. Similarly, when we see a truly good act, such as
a father sacrificing his life to save his son, we recognize
the truth of it, that what the father did, for example, was
truly the right thing, not just one subjectively good course
among many.

Truth, goodness, and beauty are like three notes of a
chord, and when they're played together we know we are
hearing something coherent and fulfilling. Or to switch metaphors, they're like the three codes to a lock. When you
turn the dial back and forth, hitting all three codes, the lock
clicks, it opens, and you're welcomed in.

That's precisely what I found in Catholicism. I discovered that in the Catholic faith these transcendentals do
converge, that the Catholic Church is worth considering
not because it's popular, progressive, or comfortable but
because it's true, good, and beautiful. In Catholicism, the
locks click and the world opens up.

But this isn't just a conversion memoir—there are lots
of those by much better writers. This book is only partly an
explanation of why I decided to become Catholic. Primarily,
it's my appeal to you, why you should consider Catholicism
yourself.

As with all appeals, this one requires an open mind.
Even just exploring the Catholic Church is an act of rebellion. But again, that makes it exciting.

Today's world is a simmering pot of rebels. Every night on the news we see fed-up citizens rebelling against dictators. Protesters fill our streets, decrying injustice. Hipsters refuse to conform to the plans of past generations. People are hungry for something radical and revolutionary.

Catholicism offers that. In fact, it's the only true rebellion left. It's not rebellious to get drunk, criticize institutions, pursue sex and money, or come out as an atheist. Everyone's doing that. Those are all mainstream. They're easy and expected. They may sometimes require a slight bit of courage, but really, everyone is following those paths, swimming along with the current.

What's truly radical is to consider a Church that billions of people have embraced throughout history but millions of people today dismiss as bigoted and outdated.

Maybe the critics are right. Maybe the Catholic Church is wrong, evil, and ugly, and the few who choose it are deluded.

But perhaps the opposite is true. Maybe in a strange and confused world, the Catholic Church looks so backward because everyone else is facing the wrong direction.

Catholicism used to be respectable. Today it's not. Choosing to be Catholic is emphatically a countercultural move.

So I invite you, through this book, to carefully consider it, if only in the spirit of rebellion. Venture into this world few people genuinely explore. Refuse to join the herd. Be willing to swim upstream.

Because when you do, you'll discover that perhaps the Catholic Church really *is* true, good, and beautiful; that it really is in harmony with our deepest desires; and that it's the rest of the world that's singing off key.

PART I

Catholicism Is True

1

Because God Exists

Like many new college students, I was hungry for truth.
My freshman year exposed me to countless new ideas, from
politics to science, economics, and religion. It was an almost
overwhelming cacophony, and I hardly knew where to start.
But I did know one thing: I wanted the truth. I didn't just
want to believe whatever my parents or professors fed me,
nor was I fine just accepting whatever made me feel good.
I wanted the truth.

The best reason to accept any belief system is because
it's true. So that's a good place to start in this exploration—
determining whether the claims of Catholicism are true.
But to arrive there we need to walk through several steps.
We can't just presume God exists or that Christianity is true
and then quickly show how Catholicism is the right expression. That wouldn't be fair. There are several stages before
that, so let's start at the very beginning. Let's start with the
question of God.

One or two hundred years ago, in most communities
throughout the world, the vast majority of people would
have taken for granted a belief in God or a higher being.

Nearly all people were religious in one way or another. But that's not true today. Over the last decade, the Western world has experienced a surge of skepticism. This has been fueled in large part by the so-called new atheists, a polemical group of scientists and philosophers who, emboldened by the Enlightenment-era skeptics who came before them, paint religion as violent, irrational, and even dangerous. These fiery doubters include bestselling authors Richard Dawkins (*The God Delusion*), Sam Harris (*Letter to a Christian Nation*), and the late Christopher Hitchens (*God Is Not Great*). Their characteristically dismissive and snarky rhetoric has gained traction, especially among young people.

But polemics are one thing; truth, another. Oftentimes, rhetoric is just a facade covering up shallow arguments. So we should push forward past the zingers and slogans and focus on the single question that really matters in this first stage: Does God exist? Catholics and other theists say yes. Atheists say no. Both of them can't be right. So how do we determine the answer? Let's examine the evidence.

EVIDENCE FOR GOD

Someone once asked the great atheist philosopher Bertrand Russell what he would say if he found himself standing before God on judgment day and God asked him, "Why didn't you believe in me?" Russell replied, "I would say, 'Not enough evidence, God! Not enough evidence!'"[2]

I run a website where millions of Catholics and atheists engage in dialogue, and I must say that's the most common refrain I hear: "Show me the evidence!" And I'm totally fine with that demand. It means the person is unwilling to accept beliefs without solid proof or support, and that's commendable. But I usually ask for some clarification: What do you mean when you say you want *evidence*? In the realm of science, evidence refers to observable phenomena, in the natural world, that confirm or challenge a hypothesis. This sort of evidence is inevitably something you can see, hear, touch, taste, or smell. In other words, it's empirical. And to be sure, this sort of evidence, in the context of science, is the right kind and has led to remarkable discoveries.

However, it's easy to forget that sensory evidence isn't the *only* type of evidence in our world. This is a crucially important fact. Sensory evidence is irrelevant, for example, when we consider questions of morality, meaning, or existence. You can't hear morality; you can't see meaning; and there's no way to touch existence. Likewise, sensory evidence is not the best type of evidence when considering God. God is, by definition and whether you believe he exists or not, immaterial and transcendent. That means he is not composed of physical matter, nor does he exist somewhere in our cosmos, perhaps beyond our galaxy; he exists beyond all space and time. And since that's the case, we would not expect to find direct, physical evidence of his existence in our world.

It's not just that we *haven't yet* found such evidence, though it may exist. It's that such evidence is impossible, even in principle. Does that mean it's impossible to show God exists? Not necessarily. It simply means that science isn't the right tool, nor is scientific evidence the right sort of evidence, to settle the God question. Just as a metal detector isn't the right instrument to settle moral questions, we need other tools to probe the existence of God.

One such tool is philosophy. Philosophy is concerned with some of life's biggest issues, from beauty to morality, existence, and free will. It allows us to explore realities that can't be detected through our senses and is therefore a much more useful tool in the quest for God.

So let's return to our original question. Is there any evidence for God? Many people certainly think so, but it's a different type of evidence than we may be used to. Instead of physical, sensory evidence, these thinkers point to arguments and logical deductions to prove their case. They've identified no less than twenty arguments for God, arguments that range from the clear and simple to the super complex.[3] Some of the arguments appeal to emotion or history; others depend on reason and experience.

We can approach the God question from many angles, and there's no one best way. But when I began seriously studying God, I did find some of the arguments stronger than others. In fact, three arguments stuck out to me, and I thought the evidence supporting them was overwhelming.

Before we dive into a few of these twenty arguments, though, I should add one more note. If terms such as *arguments* or *evidence* rub you the wrong way, it may be helpful to instead consider these as clues. Think of them as clues that converge and point to a common conclusion, much as road signs collectively guide you to a specific destination.

(Road signs don't *prove* the destination exists but show clear the way.) That's exactly what these arguments and evidence are: signposts to God. So let's look at each of them.

Clue 1: The Universe

We might as well start with the largest and most spectacular evidence that God exists, namely, the universe itself. The universe encompasses all energy, matter, space, and time. Despite its unfathomable size, it's easy to take the universe for granted. After all, we live in it and are surrounded by it every day. But in our most reflective moments, when faced with its staggering size and scope, we're led to wonder, Where did all this come from? Why does the universe exist? Why is there something rather than nothing?

From ancient times, people have posited some god or gods as the answer. This isn't just a Christian or Jewish idea. Early Greek thinkers such as Aristotle devised proofs for God based on the universe's existence. These proofs have been refined over the centuries to become simpler and clearer. Let's take a look at one popular formulation, known as the Kalam argument. Its name comes from the medieval Islamic theologian who first formulated it.

The Kalam argument is deceptively simple and runs like this:

> Premise 1: Everything that begins to exist has a cause.
> Premise 2: The universe began to exist.
> Conclusion: The universe has a cause.

The first premise is common sense and almost nobody denies it. It means that nothing just springs into existence randomly and without cause. For if that were the case, then our world would be a wild spree of things popping into existence like magic—only it would be worse than magic, since with magic you at least have a magician who pulls rabbits out of hats![4] But in a world that violated this first premise, you'd get rabbits popping in and out of being without even magicians or hats. Very few sane people believe the world works this way, and so pretty much all of us agree with this first premise.

The next premise is more controversial, or at least it used to be. For centuries, most scientists believed that the universe was eternal—it had always existed in the past. This conveniently avoided a universal beginning, which would imply a creation moment. But over the last hundred years, new discoveries from the big bang to quantum cosmology have produced a stunning reversal on this point. The scientific consensus today is that the universe had a beginning, and it occurred roughly 13.7 billion years ago. How sure are we about this? In the words of cosmologist Alexander Vilenkin, speaking at a colloquium for Stephen Hawking's seventieth birthday, "All the evidence we have says that the universe had a beginning."[5] It's extremely rare for a scientist to speak with this measure of conclusiveness. It's not just that *some* of the evidence points to a beginning, or even the *majority* of evidence, but that *all* of the evidence points this way. Vilenkin elaborated, "It is said that an argument is what convinces reasonable men and a proof is what it takes to convince even an unreasonable man. With the proof now in place, cosmologists can no longer hide behind the possibility of a past-eternal universe. There is no escape: they have to face the problem of a cosmic beginning."[6] (There are also strong philosophical reasons to think the universe must have had a beginning, but we won't get into those here.)

So the first two premises are generally accepted by common people and scientists alike. But if that's the case, the conclusion logically follows. If everything that begins to exist has a cause, and the universe began to exist, then it must have had a cause. This is required by logic.

But that leads us to natural follow-up questions: What is that cause? What's it like? What could have been responsible for causing the whole universe? Well, for starters, it couldn't have been anything *within* the universe, or even the universe itself, since things can't cause themselves to exist. (Just as your arm couldn't cause *you* to come into existence; before you existed, there was no arm!) This means the cause must be something beyond the universe, beyond all matter, energy, space, and time. In other words, it must be transcendent (beyond the universe), immaterial (beyond matter and space), and eternal (beyond time), and to create something so massively complex as the universe, it must have been tremendously powerful and intelligent.

A transcendent, immaterial, eternal, supremely powerful, intelligent cause of the universe—what does that sound like to you? There are only a few possibilities. Perhaps the cause was something abstract, such as the laws of physics, numbers, or mathematical functions. But those won't work since, to use a bit of technical language, they're causally inert. They either *describe* reality or *represent* abstract concepts, but they don't *cause* things to happen. For instance, the law of gravity *describes* the forces between objects, such as a ball falling to the earth, but the law itself doesn't *cause* the ball to fall. It only describes what happens. It's not the law but the earth's force that is actually responsible for the falling ball. Likewise, the number seven is a helpful mathematical concept, but it doesn't *cause* anything to happen and certainly can't bring something into existence.

There's only one plausible option then, only one solution that accounts for all the scientific and philosophical evidence and makes sense of the universe's existence. That would be God.

Now admittedly, this proof for God is abstract. It doesn't generate the warm, personal faith you might derive from prayer or other religious experiences. And it doesn't prove the fullness of God, especially attributes that we could only know if God revealed them to us, such as that God is love or is a Trinity of persons. It doesn't show that Catholicism, Judaism, or Mormonism is true.

But it does present a substantial slice of God, a slice far too thick for any atheist to accept. It proves the truth of theism and thus helps us move to the next stage in our exploration.

Clue 2: Morality

Before getting to that stage, though, let's look at another clue to God. The universe is probably the most overwhelming line of evidence. But another clue strikes closer to home: morality.

What is right and wrong? Have you ever considered that question? It's one that has beguiled humans since our earliest days, and we've seen all sorts of answers. Some say morality is whatever brings the most happiness to the most people. Others claim we act rightly when we treat others the way we want to be treated. Still others claim might makes right, that morality is just shaped by whoever is in charge, whoever has the power.

But when we consider morality as a clue pointing toward God, we're not so much interested in *which* moral framework is correct but in the simple fact that almost all people agree there exists *some* moral standard that we're obliged to follow.

If you need proof of this, just look at young children. Even toddlers understand the idea of rights. They shout, "That's mine!" or get upset when brothers and sisters are unfairly rewarded. There's a basic moral logic that seems innate.

For another example, try cutting ahead in a long line. Brace yourself for wrath that even Dante didn't fathom: "Hey, what do you think you're doing? You can't skip! It's wrong! We've been waiting here!"

We all experience an innate sense that some acts are just right and some acts are just wrong—even if we subtly disagree about *which* acts fall into each category.

Yet that's not all. We also experience moral duties. It's not just that we see certain actions as right or wrong; it's that we feel compelled to do the right actions and avoid the wrong ones. Many people call this our conscience. We feel as if an invisible voice compels us to act in certain good

ways, even if they go against our inclinations, and even if
they're socially unpopular. For instance, something compels us not to punch the man who insults our family or
friends even though every urge in our body says we should.
Something beyond us, or within us but distinct from us,
constantly insists how we *ought* to behave.

Most of us agree with these two facts, that we experience
moral values and moral duties. We have years of experience,
years of evidence to back them up. But there's one more
interesting facet about these values and duties: they often
seem *objective*. They originate in something beyond human
feeling and opinion. For instance, it is an objective fact that
we should not torture children. This is not just our personal
opinion, and it's not a moral fashion that changes over time,
that is true today but perhaps false tomorrow. It's true at all
times, for all people, without exception. This doesn't mean
a few people, or even a few cultures, won't be mistaken
about that fact. But in those cases, we don't just say they
have a different preference, as if the child torturers just prefer chocolate instead of vanilla. No, we say they are wrong,
emphatically wrong, and morally insane. (In fact, it's only
because some acts *are* objectively wrong that we're able to
look back through history and pass moral judgment, to say
with confidence that human sacrifice and ethnic genocide
were wrong even though some cultures happily embraced
them at the time. The fact of their wrongness remained even
though people were mistaken about the fact.)

So we all have moral values, we all experience moral
duties via our conscience, and we know that at least some

of these values and duties are objective. They aren't just personal preferences, such as our favorite type of music or ice cream, but are real objective features of reality.

But if all of that is true, we must ask ourselves: Where do these objective moral facts come from? What grounds them? If there's a moral law that binds us, what or who gives it that authority? Where's the lawgiver behind the law?

Once again, there are only a few possibilities. Either these moral values and duties come from nature, from us humans, or they have a transcendent source. They couldn't have come from nature, since as the famous atheist David Hume noted, nature only shows us what *is*; it doesn't tell us how something *ought* to behave (this is the famous "is-ought" problem in philosophy). For instance, it's a fact that if I offer to give my wife a break and take care of our children by myself for a day, it will make her happy. But that doesn't necessarily mean I *ought* to do that. The only way to get from the *is* of that fact to the *ought* is by smuggling in a hidden premise, namely, that I ought to do what makes my wife happy, a fact I certainly agree with but can't derive from nature alone. Nature, by itself, can never tell us what we *ought* to do.

But what about evolution? Couldn't evolution ground our morality? Unfortunately, no, for the same reason. Evolution may show which moral behaviors lead to survival (another *is*), but it doesn't bind us to act in a certain way (an *ought*). We're under no obligation to behave in ways that lead to survival, unless we happen to choose that for our goal, a goal that others are under no obligation to share.

Again, even atheists such as David Hume widely recognize this, that objective moral duties can't be grounded in nature.

What about society or human opinion? Don't we all just collectively decide what's moral? The problem with that conclusion is that both society in general and humans in particular are ultimately subjective. Their opinions change and their moral moods shift. Therefore, it's impossible for society in general or humans in particular to serve as an objective moral standard, the unchanging pattern by which to measure our moral performance. We also see how this fails by looking through history. If morality just depended on the common consensus, then we would have no basis on which to denounce misguided moralities of the past, such as Nazi views on Jews or early American views on slavery, both of which were held by consensus. We need some objective ground *beyond* human opinion.

Thus, as before, we're left with only one plausible explanation: God. Rather than nature, individuals, or society, it is God who is the locus of moral goodness since he is the embodiment of goodness itself. Once again, this explanation makes sense of all the available evidence. Why do we experience innate moral values? We were created by God with an innate knowledge of his natural law; to use biblical language, the law of God was "written on our hearts." Why do we sense moral duties? God created us with a specific purpose, in part to live a good life and avoid a bad one, because only the good life produces true happiness. Why are these moral values and duties objective? God is their unchanging source. God doesn't bend or evolve as does everything else in our world, be it nature, society, or personal opinion.

So it seems our moral intuition provides another strong clue to God. It shows that some perfect, transcendent standard of goodness exists beyond our universe, grounding our moral values and duties. The cause of our universe is not only transcendent, immaterial, eternal, and supremely powerful and intelligent. He is also good.

Clue 3: Reason

We've now seen two pretty large clues to God. But there's another good reason to think God exists, and it happens to be reason itself.

Atheists often champion reason over and against religion. Just consider any skeptical website, the annual "Reason Rally" held in Washington, DC, or the Richard Dawkins Foundation for Reason and Science. And to be sure, reason is obviously good. We all yearn to be people of reason who use logic and sound judgment to make rational decisions. So I join with skeptics and agree we should decry any and all irrational religion.

That said, we must ask whether reason is actually opposed to religious belief. Is it true that we are less religious as we become more reasonable? Well, as it turns out, quite the opposite can be true. Two converging arguments together make a case that reason, far from disproving God, actually points toward him.

The first argument focuses on the intelligibility of our world. That's a fancy way of saying that our universe is structured in a way that we can actually understand and model it. Consider the elegant mathematical framework undergirding our universe: this framework is not just beautiful and well ordered; it's actually understandable—it's coherent. We're able to wrap our minds around significant parts of it.

But why is this the case? It certainly didn't have to be so. Considering all the possible ways our universe could have existed, an intelligible universe is extremely unlikely. Far more probable would be a disorderly chaos. And yet, here we are. Why *is* our world so orderly and intelligible? Perhaps it's just due to chance. Maybe we just won the cosmic jackpot against almost incomprehensible odds. But that seems wildly unlikely. It seems instead that the deck was stacked, that our world happens to be intelligible against all odds because it was *intended* to be that way.

Compared to an explanation due to chance, the Christian answer makes far more sense. Christians hold that the world was designed by a supreme intelligence, which imbued the world with intelligent structure. Our universe didn't dumbly emerge by chance, they say, but was designed, given order, and marked by intelligibility. The fact that we can understand and make sense of the universe is a clue that someone planned it to be that way.

A second argument from reason is one I found even more compelling during my exploration of God. It isn't so much a positive proof for God as much as an argument *against* a world without God. Suppose, as many people believe today, that God doesn't exist and the world just blindly evolved over millions of years, beginning with simple biological organisms and building to our complex human brains, all without supernatural aid. That narrative is extremely common; it's the prevailing view in our schools and popular culture.

But if that account is true, what justification do we have for trusting our brains? In other words, if everything within us evolved, including our minds and our use of reason, why should we believe those faculties work? Why believe they are aimed at finding truth rather than mere survival (these are two different things)? The truth is we *don't* have good justification. In fact, if atheistic evolution were true, it would be far more likely that our brains would evolve into blobs of randomly firing neurons rather than coherent thinking devices.

We're left with two alternatives: we can either accept unguided, blind evolution, or we can accept our ability to reason—but not both. We can't *reasonably* accept unguided evolution. For if we hold to it, then we have no good reason to trust our reason (which would make us, by definition, insane). However, most of us know we're not insane; we know we can reason, and that requires some ground, some explanation, for believing that our minds are capable of apprehending true beliefs. Once again, Christians have a very logical proposal: that an all-intelligent God created humankind with the capacity to reason as he does. How could God do this? God, classically understood, is a divine mind, the source of all reason, and the supreme intelligence behind the cosmos. This again seems to make the best sense of our evidence. Believing in God doesn't make you anti-intellectual or antireason. Quite the opposite: God is the only plausible justification for reason itself.

We'll have to stop with these three clues—the universe, morality, and reason—but there are several other signposts to God. For example, many people have recognized God's existence after a powerful experience in nature or during prayer. Still others have found him in community, by reading the Bible, or through the impressive witness of other people. But I chose these three because they have the advantage of being *objective* clues to God. They're admittedly a bit heady, but they are clues that anyone can examine and consider, regardless of background or religious experience.

Believing in God is only the first step though. Billions of people believe in God without being Catholic, so that can't be enough to show Catholicism is true. If Catholicism really is true, then after proving God's existence we're next confronted with the question of religion, not *which* religion is correct but *why* we should follow any religion at all. Does religion matter? Why not just believe in God and hope for the best? Why not be spiritual but not religious and pray however we feel?

2

Because We Need Religion

When the History Channel debuted *Vikings*, a historical drama about Ragnar Lothbrok and his raids on England, I doubt the station could have imagined how successful it would be. The show was an immediate hit. Millions tuned in, and it quickly became the channel's most popular program. People love the truth-hungry Ragnar and his unexpected friendship with Athelstan, a Catholic monk. Throughout the series, the two wrestle with profound questions about God (and the gods), worship, sacrifice, and the afterlife. Several other characters display strong religious dimensions, from the Viking shipbuilder and mystic Floki to Ragnar's brother, Rollo, who is actually baptized Christian (for political reasons), and even the English king Ecbert, a shrewd but hypocritical Christian who reveals religion's dark side.

To be sure, all of this is probably *not* what attracts people to *Vikings*. They likely tune in for the epic battle scenes and intriguing family drama—and, admittedly, there is much to enjoy. But when you press on, you're left with a surprising fact: almost every person in *Vikings* is religious. This is remarkable in today's world. Flip through most TV shows and you'll struggle to find another that predominantly features religious characters. But *Vikings* does. Whether it's the Norse warriors offering animal (and human) sacrifices before battle, the English leaders who spend time in prayer and eucharistic adoration, or the French Catholics who charge into battle holding the relics of a saint, every person, in one way or another, realizes there is something more to this life than the plainly material. Whether Norse, English, or French, they sense a transcendent dimension that we can and should tap into, one powerful enough to even shape events on earth.

Of course, this impulse is nothing new. It didn't start with *Vikings* or its historical counterparts. Most people throughout history, over thousands of years, have not only believed in God or gods but also wrestled with how best to worship and relate to them. In a word, they sought religion.

But what exactly is religion? Don't automatically think of wooden pews, arbitrary rules, and corrupt clerics. That's the view taken by popular YouTuber Jefferson Bethke, whose viral video "Why I Hate Religion, But Love Jesus" garnered more than thirty million views. For him, "the word *religion* is pretty much synonymous with hypocrisy, legalism, self-righteousness, and self-justification."

But that's not religion—that's distorted religion, and who wouldn't gladly reject it? Religion simply means a set of beliefs and practices that connect one to a transcendent realm. Typically, religion involves a formalized way of worship, such as rubrics for animal sacrifice or liturgical customs. It usually also includes shared beliefs, such as those found in creeds or scriptures.

Yet why should all that matter? Why is it better to embrace religion rather than nothing? Well, one reason, as people have intuited up and down the ages, is that it ensures we worship the right God or gods in the right way, offering a proven way to connect with a world beyond this one. From this perspective, religion serves as a stabilizing force in the quest for God, making sure we stay on the best path.

Throughout history, people have known that whenever we're left to figure out life's Big Questions on our own, such as what to believe, who or what to worship, and how to behave morally, we often arrive at wrong answers. We inevitably shape our religious beliefs to fit our personal preferences, rather than the other way around. We choose spiritual practices that are convenient and comfortable but may not be most effective to tap into the divine world. This is why most people throughout history have seen religion as helpful, not oppressive. They understood that religion is a desperately needed guide, an admission that our collective spiritual experiences, across space and time, are more reliable than one's own solitary pursuits.

Admittedly, this view of religion—as more a good than a scourge—is not a popular one today. Religion has a worse reputation than perhaps ever before. In fact, *the* major religious story over the past ten years, at least in the Western

world, is the rise of the so-called nones. These are people
who when asked which religion they identify with, check
the "none" box (researchers also sometimes call them the
"unaffiliated"). From 2007 to 2014, the percentage of American "nones" soared from 16 percent to 23 percent.[7] That
7 percent gain, which represents around twenty million
people, was more than five times higher than the gain of
any other group. The "nones" are sweeping away religious
belief—and fast. When we look just at millennials, those
born between the 1980s and early 2000s, we learn that
roughly 35 percent are religiously unaffiliated (compared
to just 16 percent who are Catholic). In other words, young
people are now *twice* as likely to identify as "none" (nonreligious) than as Catholic.[8] In what researchers at San Diego
State University described as "the largest study ever conducted on changes in Americans' religious involvement,"
they found that "millennials are the least religious generation of the last six decades, and possibly in the nation's
history."[9]

Religion may have drenched the historical Viking culture. It may have been popular throughout most other centuries. But it's fading quickly today.

SPIRITUAL BUT NOT RELIGIOUS

Interestingly, very few of the "nones" identify as atheist or
agnostic. Most still claim to be "spiritual but not religious."
This usually means that although they eschew a specific

religion, they still agree there's a spiritual dimension to the world, something more than mere matter.

This is of course good. But the problem is that when we cast off religion, we refuse a major source of help in exploring this spiritual world. We might read spiritual books or seek out gurus, but ultimately our exploration is still self-determined and thus self-restraining.

Consider, for example, someone who claims to be "scientific but not into scientific laws and rules." They might agree that science offers incredible facts about the world, but they refuse to read any science textbooks or journals (too dry and abstract, full of rules and maxims), and they ignore Galileo, Newton, or Darwin (too ancient and out of touch). We would naturally be wary. We would say, How can you be scientific but ignore science? By ignoring the history and tradition of this whole field, all of the geniuses and their discoveries, you're missing out on a tremendous amount of knowledge. These founders and fathers who have gone before you have cleared the way. They've found scientific dead ends that you shouldn't waste your time treading, and they've also paved new roads that remain promising. What they offer are shortcuts to keep you from wasting your time and attention. Follow them! Lean on their wisdom! If you're truly scientific, you should love science too, availing yourself of all the help science can provide!

Now switch "science" for "religion" and you'll get the point we're driving at here. Through its doctrines and creeds, customs and liturgies, religion offers the collective wisdom of all who have gone before us. Embracing religion means listening to what G. K. Chesterton called "the democracy of the dead," the shared consensus among our ancestors that says religion is a helpful thing.

But if religion is generally good, does this mean *all* religions are good and true? Of course not. Each religion may be wholly or partially true and helpful, or perhaps not at all. We have to examine them individually, and we'll approach that in the next chapter. But it does mean that religion, in general, offers a helpful way forward in the spiritual life beyond fickle guesswork and feelings and is therefore worth considering.

FROM POINTLESS RULES TO HELPFUL RELIGION

I'm a millennial, and it was in college that I first began seriously asking religious questions. I joined a Methodist ministry where we read the Bible, discussed it in small groups, and prayed together every week. But while I'm sure the ministry didn't intend this, it was easy to think we were spiritual pioneers, forging our own paths forward. Instead of relying on dusty old creeds and fickle institutions, we sat in circles and wondered, What does this Bible verse mean to *you*? How do *you* understand it?

That was fine, and in a way it was exciting. But over time, I became disenchanted with the approach. I remember feeling lost and thinking, If God really wanted us to know the truth, why would he force each of us to figure out these religious questions on our own? Wouldn't that put huge numbers of people at a disadvantage? What about people who have difficulty reading? What about those without the time or ability to study long books and commentaries? Would God really just leave everything up to each individual to figure out, despite the vast range of cognitive capabilities? It just didn't seem like a great plan.

And then I discovered Catholicism. As a senior in college, as I began exploring this strange new system that took a dramatically different view on these questions, I was surprised by what I found. The Catholic Church seemed to suggest, You are not on your own. Our tradition, which stretches back for thousands of years, holds vast treasures of wisdom and insight, which God has revealed through scripture and unpacked through saints, popes, and bishops and which has been safeguarded and passed down through generations—all for you. Whether you're the simplest peasant or the most brilliant scholar, here is a proven roadmap to God that has helped countless people find him.

I found this deeply liberating, even before gauging whether that tradition was actually true. It began to change my mind about religion. As I began examining each of the Church's beliefs and rules, the sense grew in me that religion was actually helpful and life-giving rather that stultifying.

One example of this process was the strange Catholic practice of abstaining from meat on Fridays during Lent (and, ideally, throughout the rest of the year). I remember thinking this was incredibly odd. Why would Catholics do that? Why would you voluntarily give up one particular food group on one particular day of the week? What does that possibly have to do with God? Isn't that just one more example of an unnecessary, pointless, oppressive religious rule that the Church cooked up?

It was easy to be dismissive about it—until I tried to give up meat. I then discovered a couple things. First, giving up meat was far more difficult than I thought it would be. Inevitably, when Friday rolled around, I would have sudden cravings for chicken or steak that conveniently never emerged on other days. It became a real sacrifice. Second, I learned that when you abstain from meat, or fast from something else, there's a mystical hole that opens up deep within you, some emptiness that emerges. To risk a cliché, it's as if you open a spiritual vacuum. What you've willfully eschewed demands satisfaction, and as I came to see, that's where the wisdom of this practice comes in. The Church doesn't encourage people to give up meat so that Catholics can pig out on lobster or fried fish instead. The aim is to open up space for God, fulfilling our earthly hunger with spiritual sustenance (which explains the Friday timing: Friday coincides with the day of Jesus' sacrificial death on the Cross). When you feel the pang of desire for meat, it's a helpful reminder that you're wired for God; as St. Augustine opines, "Our hearts are restless until they rest in you." Only God can fulfill the deepest hungers of our hearts, hungers that even the choicest steak will leave unsatisfied.

So in the end, this seemingly pointless religious rule helped invigorate my spiritual life. I came to see giving up meat as a tool for spiritual progress rather than an arbitrary demand.

And this wasn't an isolated example. I experienced this over and over throughout my conversion. Each doctrine or practice that I looked at, most of which I considered religious burdens, turned out to be powerful aids in my spiritual life. I eventually learned to see religion not as a threat but as a tremendous help.

RIVERS AND REFEREES

John Henry Newman, a famous nineteenth-century English clergyman, came to the same conclusion. He compared religious teachings to the sturdy banks of a river. Suppose you have a river with hard, sharp banks on either side. The sturdy banks will cause the river to move forward with great power and verve. But if you soften up the banks, the water will slow down. Remove the banks altogether and the raging river will devolve into a large, lazy lake.[10]

That describes much of our culture today, doesn't it? People feel drawn to spiritual things but stuck when it comes to God—no motion, no progress. They want to become more spiritual or tap into the divine world, but they mostly feel they're just floating along without any direction. Yet that's what the "banks" of religion provide. Liturgy, rules, doctrines, and creeds aren't meant to slow down religious progress. They're the very conditions that allow it to surge.

To offer another analogy, consider a referee in a sports game. Although he's constantly halting the game to call a foul or throw a penalty flag, his goal isn't to wreck the game's progress. He's there to help it flourish. By enforcing rules that have proven to move the game forward, he's actually a great and necessary part of its success. Any child playing ball, whether in the park or in the home, knows that without a referee, things get quickly out of control. The rules become less and less enforced, disputes threaten to undermine the game, and without a clear, agreed-upon system of what's allowed, the game becomes confusing and eventually unappealing.

That's why we need religion. Clerics, priests, bishops, and popes are, in a sense, religious referees. They're not power-hungry leaders, eager to crack their doctrinal whips at wrongdoers. Instead, their primary duty is to ensure the smooth flow of the religious life.

RELIGION MAKES YOU HAPPIER AND HEALTHIER

But suppose you're still on the fence. You understand why some people are attracted to religion. You're happy for your mom, grandma, or people living thousands of years ago who were deeply devout, but the thought of *you* shifting from "spiritual but not religious" to "spiritual *and* religious" makes you uneasy. Well, here's one more argument in its favor, and it's a purely practical one: religion makes you happier and healthier.

This fact is one of the most well documented in sociology. A large body of research has tied religious belief to well-being. For example, Nick Spencer runs the religion and society think tank Theos, and his group trawled through nearly 140 studies from the past thirty years to see whether there were any verifiable, positive outcomes to being religious. They concluded, "The correlation between religion and well-being is pretty strong, wherever you go and whatever kind of religion you are talking about. There are a few outlier studies, some inconclusive, some negative, but the weight of the evidence is overwhelmingly positive."[11]

According to the research, religious people have lower rates of mental health issues, less depression, stronger marriages and better-behaved children, and longer and healthier lives, including lower blood pressure and stress; they also exhibit much lower rates of domestic abuse, addiction, and crime. Those are objective outcomes verified by several studies. But even subjective data confirm this connection. For example, in a large recent study by the Pew Research Center, 40 percent of religious US adults say they are "very happy," compared to just 29 percent who don't identify as religious.[12]

Interestingly, the Theos research also found that religious *affiliation* had a pretty weak correlation with well-being. In other words, it doesn't really matter *which* religion you choose, at least in terms of happiness. You'll experience more well-being with *any* religion. (Note that this doesn't mean all religions are equally *true*, as we'll see in the next chapter, just that they make people equally happy and healthy.)

So for all these reasons and more, religion is a good thing. If our goal is to get at the truth—the truth about God, the universe, and our purpose within it—we can use all the help we can get. That includes the help provided by religion, a stabilizing force that has helped billions of people connect with God and progress in the spiritual life.

But once again, we're faced with a natural question: Which religion? It would be wrong to just assume that when we say "religion" we mean "Christianity," just because that's the most popular religion in America and in the world today. How do we know that's the right one, the religion with the most truth? That's a great question, and it's the one we'll turn to next.

3

Because Jesus Is God

I remember the sign. It forced me to do a double take because it was so strange. There, towering high, were four different images with names underneath: Zeus, Poseidon, Santa Claus, and . . . Jesus. A big caption read, "What myths do you see? 37 million Americans know myths when they see them." Beneath it was the logo for the American Atheists society.

The insinuation was clear. Just as we have no historical evidence for Zeus, Poseidon, or Santa Claus, we have none for Jesus. He's just one more legend among many, and since we reject those first three myths, we should reject Jesus too.

Now even though I disagree with the billboard's main point, I do appreciate how it drives at the central religious question: Who is Jesus? So far in this book, we've explored strong evidence for God and good reasons to be open to religion. The next obvious step is to ask, which religion? And to answer that question, as the atheists rightfully intuit, we must consider Jesus of Nazareth.

When we look at the world's major religions—Christianity, Islam, Hinduism, Buddhism, Sikhism, and Judaism—we find that what ultimately divides them is their views about Jesus. To put it simply, Christians are convinced that Jesus is God. Every other religion thinks he is something far less.

So who is Jesus really?

THE FORGOTTEN ALTERNATIVE

C. S. Lewis, the beloved Christian writer, made famous the "liar, lunatic, Lord" argument for Jesus' divinity. He suggested that when you look at the strange, radical things Jesus said and did, in which he seemed to speak and act in the very person of God, we're left with only three options: Jesus was a liar, someone who knowingly deceived his followers by pretending to be God. He was a lunatic, someone who genuinely believed he was God but was badly deluded. Or he was Lord, God in human form and thus worthy of our praise and devotion.

But as many skeptics point out, there's a fourth option that Lewis didn't explicitly consider. What if Jesus never claimed to be God? For one thing, weren't the biblical accounts of Jesus written centuries after the events they record, and thus weren't they likely manipulated or warped in transmission? And even if the Bible is reliable, it doesn't seem to show Jesus ever claiming to be God. He never outright says, "I am God," or explicitly makes that association.

To be honest, I hadn't heard these objections before starting college. They never popped up during my childhood, and even after becoming spiritually curious in college, I just took it for granted that the Bible was trustworthy. I signed up for an Introduction to the New Testament course my senior year, hoping that would spur my faith on even more. But it had almost the opposite effect. It cast a dark cloud of skepticism. My professor, who was not a Christian, seemed to delight in undermining the naive faith of her students, particularly by casting doubt on the gospel accounts of Jesus' life. (It didn't help that the textbook she required for our class was written by Bart D. Ehrman, one of today's foremost biblical skeptics.)

Her objections shook me at first. Until that class, I never knew that some scholars doubted the Bible's reliability or considered Jesus to be little more than an itinerant prophet. The class forced me to seriously wrestle with these issues. I began reading books and scouring the work of scholars. Eventually, I came full circle on both objections and came to see not only that the Bible offers a reliable picture of Jesus but also that Jesus indeed claimed to be God.

Let's take a look at some of these main objections. To begin, is the Bible reliable? Specifically, do the four New Testament accounts of Jesus accurately reflect his life and teachings? Many skeptics say no, and they have what seems to be good reason: we have zero original manuscripts of the New Testament. And the copies we do have were compiled long after Jesus' death—decades or even a century later.

But while it's true the earliest manuscripts we have are copies of copies, that isn't a huge problem. Why? We're extremely confident in the accuracy of those copies, due to their vast number and diversity. The more copies we have, the better we can compare them to one another to confirm what the originals were like. And the number of New Testament copies is unprecedented. The New Testament survived in more unique manuscripts (full or partial texts) than any work in classical antiquity. For instance, we have only six hundred surviving manuscripts of Homer's *Iliad*, but of the New Testament we have more than five thousand cataloged so far. With that many copies, originating at different times and from numerous regions, we can affirm, with near certainty, what the originals contained.

Other clues give us more confidence about the New Testament. Nearly twenty different *non-Christian* writers cover the life of Christ, including the famous Jewish historian Josephus, Tacitus, Pliny the Younger, and the emperor Trajan. Although some accounts suggest Jesus was actually a wizard or sorcerer who led Israel astray, what's interesting is that none of them doubt he did marvelous things or was crucified and raised from the dead. They simply attribute his power to a different source (e.g., magic instead of divinity).

In addition to that extrabiblical confirmation, we also have the well-attested historical fact that Jesus' followers genuinely believed he performed miracles and was raised from the dead. If they made up these stories, as some skeptics accuse, why would they do that? What did they have to gain? Tradition holds that eleven of Jesus' twelve apostles were tortured and killed for their testimony that Jesus rose from the dead (only John was spared death, but his consolation was being plunged into boiling oil in Rome's Colosseum). If the apostles knew their testimony was false, if they knew they had made it up, then why go to their deaths for it? People often die for beliefs they *think* are true but are really false, such as terrorists who fly planes into buildings because they think it will earn them seventy-two virgins in heaven. But people don't die for a belief they *know* is false, which would have to be the case with Jesus' apostles.

What's more, the "legend" charge doesn't hold from a literary perspective. In addition to making famous the "liar, lunatic, Lord" argument, C. S. Lewis served as the chair of Mediaeval and Renaissance Literature at Cambridge, where he was one of the world's leading experts on myth and legend. He wrote:

> As a literary historian, I am perfectly convinced that whatever else the Gospels are they are not legends. I have read a great deal of legend and I am quite clear that they are not the same sort of thing. They are not artistic enough to be legends. From an imaginative point of view they are clumsy, they don't work up to things properly.
>
> Most of the life of Jesus is totally unknown to us, as is the life of anyone else who lived at that time, and no people building up a legend would allow that to be so. Apart from bits of the Platonic dialogues, there are no conversations that I know of in ancient literature like the Fourth Gospel [the Gospel of John]. There is nothing, even in modern literature, until about a hundred years ago when the realistic novel came into existence.

In the story of the woman taken in adultery
we are told Christ bent down and scribbled in the
dust with His finger. Nothing comes of this. No
one has ever based any doctrine on it. And the
art of inventing little irrelevant details to make
an imaginary scene more convincing is a purely
modern art. Surely the only explanation of this
passage is that the thing really happened? The
author put it in simply because he had seen it.[13]

Finally, there's no example anywhere in history of a
great myth or legend arising around a historical figure and
being generally believed within thirty years of that figure's
death. Scholars disagree precisely on the dating of the four
gospels, but the general range is somewhere between AD
50 and 100. More importantly, the letters of Paul, which
predate all of the gospels and which forcefully proclaim
that Jesus is God, are typically dated to the AD 40s or 50s.
Assuming the consensus view that Jesus died around AD
33, that means within a handful of years (not decades or
centuries), large numbers of people were already convinced
Jesus had risen from the dead. Again, if this were a myth or
legend, it would be nearly impossible for it to develop that
quickly, especially when numerous eyewitnesses were still
around. If fictitious healings and miracles were attributed
to Jesus, or if he merely died and rotted in his grave, plenty
of people would have corrected popular legends about this
miracle worker who defied death. But we have no examples
of any of that.

The fact is that every early century account of Jesus, whether from believer or skeptic, or from Jew or non-Jew, confirms that the New Testament narratives are reliable. Even if some of the minor details differ between the accounts, the combined picture offers an accurate account of what Jesus said and did.

THE GOD MAN

But that just answers the first objection. The Bible may be trustworthy, at least in its general accounts about Jesus. But in those accounts, did Jesus actually claim to be God? Certainly, we have no record of Jesus explicitly claiming, "I am God." But there's good reason for this. Jesus unveiled his divine identity slowly over time and typically only to his close followers. He seems to have done it this way because he knew that overtly claiming to be God would make him a threat to Roman leaders. Their reaction would be swift and lethal. So Jesus instead used coded language that Jews of his day would have picked up on but the Roman authorities would have missed.

Let's briefly look at a few examples. First, in Mark's gospel, Jesus encounters a crippled man who had been lowered through the roof of a house. Jesus says, "Child, your sins are forgiven," to which the bystanders respond, "Why does this man speak that way? He is blaspheming! Who but God alone can forgive sins?" (Mk 2:5, 7). They were, of course, right. No prophet, sage, or teacher in Israel could ever forgive sins. All they could do was call people to repent and

have them beg God to forgive them. So when Jesus encountered the crippled man and presumed to forgive his sins,
the implication was clear: this man was claiming to do what
only God could do.

Next, in Matthew's gospel, Jesus says, "He who does not
love me more than his mother or father is not worthy of me"
(Mt 10:37). Can you imagine a merely human teacher saying
that? Buddha, Confucius, or Socrates might say, "You must
love *this teaching* more than even your own family," but
they would never say, "You must love *me* above all else."
Why? That would make them the greatest possible good—a
description reserved only for God. Yet once again, we see
Jesus claiming that role for himself.

Elsewhere in Matthew's gospel, Jesus says, "I say to you,
something greater than the temple is here," obviously referring to himself (Mt 12:6). As first-century Jews knew, only
God himself was greater than the Jerusalem Temple. Once
again, we see Jesus claiming divinity for himself.

Perhaps most remarkably, when Jesus says in Matthew's
gospel, almost as a tossed-off aside after his famous Sermon
on the Mount, "You have heard that it was said . . . but I
say . . ." he is implying superiority to the Torah, the ancient
Jewish scriptures. This would have alarmed the Jews, for
whom the Torah was the highest possible authority. The
only one superior to the Torah would be the author of the
Torah, namely, God himself—which is precisely what Jesus
was implying.

It's worth noting that all the affirmations above come
from what scholars call the synoptic gospels (Matthew,

Mark, and Luke). These are usually dated much earlier than the Gospel of John and thus assumed to be more reliable. But if we turn to John, we see even stronger support for the idea that Jesus claimed to be God. In that gospel Jesus says, "The Father and I are one" (Jn 10:30); "Whoever sees me sees the one who sent me" (Jn 12:45); and "Before Abraham came to be, I AM" (Jn 8:58), this latter claim assuming the divine name (I AM) for himself, a shocking move that caused Jewish leaders to rip their clothes and accuse Jesus of blasphemy. Clearly they knew what Jesus meant—he was claiming to be God.

There are many more examples, but these will suffice to show that in the gospels, when read properly through a first-century Jewish lens, Jesus indeed claimed to be God. And from our earlier exploration, we have good reason to believe these accounts are reliable. With those facts in mind, let's return to C. S. Lewis's famous trilemma. If Jesus reliably claimed to be God, then we have only three options: he's a liar, a lunatic, or Lord.

We can swiftly eliminate the first two possibilities. Was Jesus a liar? Well, even the most hardened atheists affirm that Jesus was among the most truthful, noble, and reliable people ever to have lived. To verify this, just stop a group of random people on the street and ask, "Who was the most honest man in history?" Jesus would win in a landslide. We have zero evidence to think Jesus was any sort of con man, and he had no motive to lie, nothing to gain other than a brutal, tortuous death.

But perhaps he was a lunatic. Maybe Jesus meant well but was deceived about who he was. Again, we just don't have any evidence to think Jesus was deluded or insane. The historical accounts we have present him as eminently clear thinking. He was humble, balanced, and showed remarkable clarity. He was a model of sanity.

So that leaves us, finally, with only one logical conclusion, and it's the one that billions of people have reached over the centuries: Jesus really is who he claims to be, God in human form. But for most believers in Jesus, there's one more piece of evidence—the strongest piece of all—that solidifies his claim to divinity.

THE STRONGEST PROOF THAT JESUS IS GOD

As a young college student, if you had asked me whether I "believed in the Resurrection," I probably would have answered, "Sure." But I would have meant that in the same way that I "believed in democracy" or "believed in Martin Luther King Jr." It would have been an affirmation that the Resurrection was a powerful, meaningful event that brings hope and joy to many people—I believed in it because I supported it, I thought it helped people.

But once I began questioning my own beliefs and embarked on a thorough study of Christianity, I was forced to ask myself, Sure, Jesus' resurrection may be inspiring. Sure, it may help people. But did it really happen? Is it a historical fact? Is it true?

This is perhaps *the* pivotal religious question, at least when deciding among different religions: Did Jesus rise from the dead? If yes, then Christianity is true and Jesus is God. If no, then Christianity is false and Jesus is, at best, just one great teacher among many. St. Paul, one of the earliest Christian leaders, articulated the stakes well: "If Christ has not been raised, then empty [too] is our preaching; empty, too, your faith" (1 Cor 15:14). Everything hinges on the Resurrection.

So why do Christians believe that Jesus rose from the dead? Some believe it through personal intuition or experience. They may say, as the old hymn goes, "You ask me how I know he lives? He lives within my heart!" This may suffice at the personal level, but the problem is it's subjective and won't convince anyone else. You and I have no way to adjudicate whether such a person is really experiencing the risen Jesus or is just deluded. What you and I want is objective evidence of Jesus' resurrection. We want evidence that is independent of personal feelings or experience. Fortunately, Christianity, unlike many other religions, is rooted in history and thus can be investigated historically. We have an extraordinary amount of historical testimony to the life and death of Jesus, including four independent accounts containing eyewitness testimony and numerous other historical references.

When I started looking into the Resurrection, I assumed most scholars had already refuted it. I knew that many simplistic Christians still believed in it, in a literal way, but I didn't think real thinkers took it seriously. I was stunned to learn that a surge of new scholarship has provided more support for the Resurrection than at any other point in history. Specifically, the majority of New Testament scholars today, believers and skeptics alike, agree on five basic historical facts about the end of Jesus' life, five facts that collectively point to the truth of the Resurrection.[14]

We don't have enough space for a full defense of each fact, but here's a brief overview.[15] First, Jesus died by crucifixion. Second, Jesus was given an honorable burial in the tomb of Joseph of Arimathea. Third, Jesus' tomb was discovered empty on the third day after his death. Fourth, several people from different backgrounds, including friends and enemies, claimed to have seen and interacted with Jesus after his death. Fifth, after these encounters, Jesus' disciples experienced a sudden and remarkable transformation— they went from being afraid and defeated to boldly proclaiming that Jesus was alive.

Again, these five facts are widely accepted by serious New Testament scholars, believers and nonbelievers alike.[16] Each fact is independently confirmed by multiple historical sources. We have stronger evidence for these facts than almost any other fact from the ancient world.

But just discovering they had wide support among scholars wasn't enough for me. I then had to wonder, what's the most plausible explanation of these facts? For instance, perhaps Jesus' followers simply made up the story of his Resurrection. Well, that scenario may explain a couple of the facts, but it wouldn't explain the empty tomb, the postmortem encounters, or the disciples' transformation. Or to take another trendy hypothesis, maybe the disciples were all hallucinating and they *thought* they saw Jesus alive after his death but really didn't. Yet that's extremely unlikely too. Besides the fact that we have no record of people ever experiencing mass hallucinations on this scale, the scenario again fails to explain all the facts, especially the empty tomb.

After weighing each popular theory, I concluded that the only one that satisfies all the facts and explains them coherently, the only one that makes sense of the evidence, is the Resurrection hypothesis—the magnificent fact that Jesus actually rose from the dead, vindicating all his previous claims to be God.

This sets Jesus apart from any other religious or mythical figure. We have no historical evidence for Zeus, Poseidon, or Santa Claus. Confucius, Moses, and Buddha never claimed to be God or rose from the dead. But Jesus is different. We know he existed as a historical person, and we have strong reasons to think he is divine, from the logic of Lewis's "liar, lunatic, or Lord" trilemma to the well-supported fact of his Resurrection.

But even that doesn't take us all the way to Catholicism. It gets us to Christianity, however. If Jesus really is God, then religions that claim Jesus is *not* God are, at least on this crucial point, deeply mistaken. They may be right about lots of other things. They may indeed contain much truth. But they're off base on this fundamental issue: Who is God, and is Jesus really God? Christianity is alone in getting the answer right.

Yet Christianity isn't equal to Catholicism. There are thousands of versions of Christianity. Catholicism is one option, but there are also Evangelical, Methodist, Anglican, nondenominational, and many other versions. So once again we find ourselves asking, which to pursue? Which is the truest expression of Christianity?

4

Because Jesus Started a Church

According to a recent poll, the funniest joke of the century happens to be a religious one:

> Once I saw this guy on a bridge about to jump.
>
> I said, "Don't do it!" He said, "Nobody loves me."
>
> I said, "God loves you. Do you believe in God?" He said, "Yes."
>
> I said, "Are you a Christian or a Jew?" He said, "A Christian."
>
> I said, "Me too! Protestant or Catholic?" He said, "Protestant."
>
> I said, "Me too! What franchise?" He said, "Baptist."
>
> I said, "Me too! Northern Baptist or Southern Baptist?" He said, "Northern Baptist."
>
> I said, "Me too! Northern Conservative Baptist or Northern Liberal Baptist?" He said, "Northern Conservative Baptist."

I said, "Me too! Northern Conservative Baptist Great Lakes Region, or Northern Conservative
Baptist Eastern Region?" He said, "Northern Conservative Baptist Great Lakes Region."

I said, "Me too! Northern Conservative Baptist
Great Lakes Region Council of 1879, or Northern
Conservative Baptist Great Lakes Region Council
of 1912?" He said, "Northern Conservative Baptist Great Lakes Region Council of 1912."

I said, "Die, heretic!" And I pushed him over.

The joke is grim but also a bit funny. And it's funny
because it's so absurd. Obviously, nobody—we hope—
would push someone over a bridge because of such a minor
religious difference. But there is a tinge of truth to it. Most of
us, whether religious or not, are aware of religious division.
We see it everywhere, not just between warring religions
but even within individual religious groups.

Christianity is no exception. Schisms and splits have
created thousands of different Christian subgroups. Of
course, this is deeply regretful for Christians, but it also
makes things difficult for seekers trying to determine which
version of Christianity is the *right* one. There are so many
to choose from!

So far in this book, we've discovered good reasons to
think God exists. Clues such as morality, reason, and the
universe itself suggest there must be a transcendent, powerful force behind it all. From there, we explored how people
throughout history have embraced religion, sensing that we
need something beyond mere spirituality; we need help to

choose the right ways to live, pray, and worship. That led to an obvious question: *Which* religion? Our search focused on the person of Jesus of Nazareth, the most critical dividing point between all religions. We zoomed in on the central question about Jesus—Is Jesus really God?—and saw that the best explanation for Jesus' radical claims and his Resurrection from the dead is that he was who he claimed to be: God in the flesh.

But that still leaves us with one final hurdle before determining whether Catholicism is true: Among the many variations of Christianity, which tradition is the right one? Catholicism or something else—maybe Evangelical, Baptist, Orthodox, or another?

Billions of Christians agree that God exists and Jesus is God. But beyond that, serious differences emerge. Some hold that the only thing that matters is that one personally knows and follows Jesus—the rest is just icing on the cake. It doesn't matter what church you belong to, whether you go to services on Sunday, or whether you participate in any sacraments, such as baptism, confession, or ordination. All that matters is that you develop a personal relationship with Jesus.

Other Christians agree that such a relationship is central but that God has more in store for his followers. They believe it's through the Church that we best know and experience Jesus, that God has prescribed how he wants us to worship him so we're not left to our own whims, and that our spiritual health depends on receiving his sacraments.

And these are just two perspectives. Within Christianity, you'll find thousands more.

It wasn't always this confusing. For the first thousand years of Christianity, the Church was relatively unified. In fact, in the year 107, the term *Catholic Church* was first used to describe the community of believers, "catholic" meaning universal or all embracing. Of course, there were small, spin-off groups, some that even gained significant influence in the Church, but for the most part, the Christian Church was unified.

However, around 1054, the Eastern Church split off from the Western Church in what's known as the Great Schism. The East severed all ties with the pope and created the first major division in Christianity. Even today, the Eastern Churches (often known collectively as Eastern Orthodoxy) remain separated from the Roman Catholic Church (called Roman because of its allegiance to the bishop of Rome, also known as the pope).

Another major blow struck five hundred years later, in the sixteenth century, when the Protestant Reformation split the Church again. This time it split Western Christianity (then primarily Catholic) apart, creating several Protestant denominations. Each new group was led by a founding reformer: Lutheranism (Martin Luther), Calvinism (John Calvin), and Anglicanism (King Henry VIII), among others. Those groups spawned even more spin-off groups, including Presbyterians, Methodists, and Baptists, contributing to the dizzying number of denominations today. How many? Most estimates are in the thousands.

So among all these Christian traditions, how can we determine which is the right one? Or if there even is a right one? Why not just be Christian and leave it at that?

WHY SO ARROGANT?

I remember having dinner with an Evangelical friend after I converted to Catholicism. At some point, he began asking questions about my decision. I shared several reasons that I had decided to become Catholic, reasons I felt were pretty compelling. But then my friend interrupted and said, "Yeah, I see where you're coming from, but—and don't take this wrong way—to me it just seems a bit arrogant to think *you've* found the true Christian religion and everyone else is completely wrong. What gives you the confidence to say that?"

I was surprised by his reaction. When exploring the Catholic Church, my primary mission was simply to follow the evidence where it led—whether it led me to become Catholic, remain Protestant, or just abandon the whole thing altogether. It had never occurred to me that by settling on one conclusion, I was rejecting, at least implicitly, all the alternatives.

As I thought more about his reaction, though, I realized that the same criticism could be leveled against *any* decision. When we settle on any truth or choice, we're implicitly rejecting many others. This isn't a bad thing; it just seems that way in our hyper-tolerant culture that has lifted open-mindedness to the level of virtue. Yet as G. K. Chesterton observed,

"Merely having an open mind is nothing. The object of opening the mind, as of opening the mouth, is to shut it again on
something solid."[17]

We can and should be open-minded about religious
questions. We should put all options on the table and consider them fairly. But such open-mindedness is the beginning, not the end, of the search. After settling the question
as best we can, it's time, to use Chesterton's image, to bite
down on it solidly and with confidence. It's no more arrogant for a Catholic to be confident in his Catholicism than
for an atheist to be confident God is imaginary, for a Baptist to be sure the pope is a fraud, or for "spiritual but not
religious" people to hold that religion is unnecessary. Even
though I, a Catholic, would now disagree with those other
positions, I would never consider them arrogant. It's not
arrogant to believe you've found the truth. It would only
be arrogant if you arrived there without good reason and
refused to weigh other alternatives.

I came to see another problem with my friend's reaction: it wasn't an accurate view of how the Catholic Church
views other forms of Christianity—or other religions. Catholics don't see the religious search as a binary, zero-sum
game where one religion is 100 percent true and the others
0 percent true. The Catholic Church maintains that while
Catholicism holds the "fullness of truth," meaning the fullness of what God has revealed directly to us about himself and the world, this doesn't mean the Catholic Church
knows *everything* about everything or that other religions
fail to teach some (or most) of that same truth.

In fact, it holds explicitly the opposite view. This is from the Catholic Church's most recent council, which is its highest form of Catholic religious teaching:

> Other religions found everywhere try to counter the restlessness of the human heart, each in its own manner, by proposing "ways," comprising teachings, rules of life, and sacred rites. The Catholic Church rejects nothing that is true and holy in these religions. She regards with sincere reverence those ways of conduct and of life, those precepts and teachings which, though differing in many aspects from the ones she holds and sets forth, nonetheless often reflect a ray of that Truth which enlightens all men.[18]

The Catholic Church indeed believes Catholicism is the fullest expression of truth on earth (which is what all other religions believe about themselves too). But it doesn't assume other religions are thus completely wrong. It draws the commonsense conclusion that other religions, to the degree they veer from the Catholic Church, offer a mixture of truth and confusion.

So it's not arrogant to conclude that one Christian tradition is truer than others, and by concluding this you're not saying that every other tradition is 100 percent wrong.

But we're still left with the question: *Which* tradition should we bite down upon? Before jumping straight to Catholicism, let's first look at America's most popular form of Christianity, namely, Protestantism.

JESUS LEFT A CHURCH, NOT A BIBLE

Taken as a whole, Protestant Christianity is the most popular religion in America. (By Protestant, I simply mean all forms of Christianity that are not Catholic or Eastern Orthodox.) America was founded by Protestant leaders and with a Protestant spirit. Because of this, Protestantism is often confused with Christianity in general. Perhaps the most prominent example involves the idea of *sola scriptura* (scripture alone), the distinctly Protestant belief that the Bible is our sole, infallible religious authority. *Sola scriptura* is the foundation for statements such as,

- If it's not in the Bible, I won't believe it.
- Give me the Word of God, not the words of men.
- That can't be true because the Bible teaches . . .

Now, appealing to the Bible isn't a bad thing. All Christians agree that the Bible is the inspired Word of God, and thus authoritative and worthy of devotion. But there are several major problems with *sola scriptura*, and thus several problems with Protestantism.

First, *sola scriptura* is self-refuting. Nowhere in the Bible will you find the idea that the Bible is all we need for religious guidance. One often-cited passage, 2 Timothy 3:16–17, says that scripture is necessary but not sufficient, just as a bat is necessary for a baseball game but is not *all* you need. *Sola scriptura* is an extra- and antibiblical idea, stemming from outside the Bible and thus undermining its own principle.

Second, *sola scriptura* fails to explain scripture itself. During the first few centuries, Christians venerated dozens of writings and accounts of Jesus, many of which were considered to be inspired by God. But which ones *really* came from God and which were frauds? Which belonged in the Bible and which didn't? The Bible itself couldn't answer that question since the Bible, as we know it today, containing the Old and New Testaments, wasn't formally compiled until the fourth century. Instead, the early communities needed an objective authority to settle the important matter. That authority was the Church, under the guidance of the pope and other bishops. To settle controversial questions such as the nature of Jesus or which books make up the Bible, the Church held councils, trusting that God gave bishops the authority to do so and would guide them to truth. Jesus said to his apostles, and thus to their successors, the bishops, "Whoever listens to you listens to me" (Lk 10:16). Thus, the very books of the Bible, which *sola scriptura* takes for granted, rely on something outside of the Bible, namely, the authority of the Church.

A final blow against *sola scriptura* is that no early Christians held this view. It's a novel idea in the history of Christianity, first proposed nearly fifteen centuries after Jesus' Resurrection. It's not something that originates with Jesus. In fact, it's an example of the man-made rules Jesus explicitly railed against.

But if Jesus didn't intend or provide a Bible to be our ultimate authority, how did he expect us to settle tough religious questions? I wondered that during my period of religious searching, and after several months, I finally found a sensible answer: he established a Church. Other than a brief scene in the Gospel of John where Jesus writes in the sand, we have no historical record of Jesus ever writing or passing down a single written word. However, he did say to Peter, his closest disciple, "You are Peter, and upon this rock I will build my church," also saying that even the powers of death would not prevail against it (Mt 16:18). You'll find these very words inscribed in seven-foot-high letters, circling the dome at St. Peter's Basilica in the Vatican. That basilica was built over the bones of the apostle Peter, a symbolic reminder that the Church Jesus began with Peter continues today in the Catholic Church.

Indeed, the Bible itself describes the Church as "the pillar and foundation of truth" (1 Tm 3:15), a title it never applies to scripture.

This was a bombshell realization for me. Clearly Jesus wanted to carry on the new kingdom he ushered into the world, but after his Resurrection he needed some way to perpetuate it. A Bible alone wouldn't suffice, for obvious reasons: it still needed to be interpreted by people. Thus, there needed to be some way to settle disputes when well-intentioned Christians read the same Bible but arrived at different interpretations. (The American founders faced a similar problem, knowing that a constitution couldn't govern society by itself. That's why they established outside authorities, such as Congress and a Supreme Court, to apply and interpret the document, respectively.)

Jesus established a Church, a living, divine institution to which he imparted his own authority, in order to carry out his mission down through the centuries, speaking and acting in his name. This Church would be led by his closest disciples, who in turn would pass on their authority to successors. Catholics call this "apostolic succession," a tracing of authority from Jesus to his disciples, bishops, and popes down through the centuries and finally to today's bishops and pope.

We're sailing into somewhat technical territory here, but the key point is this: Jesus established a Church, not a Bible, as the way to propagate his new way of life. The Bible stems from the Church. It was compiled by the Church, spread by the Church, and has been safeguarded down through history by the Church. It remains the holy, inspired Word of God. However, it's not our only source of religious guidance. The Catholic Church offers the Bible—plus more.

I came to realize that if *sola scriptura* was false, then most Protestant groups were wrong about a centrally revered principle. That was a huge strike against them, in my book.

But *sola scriptura* wasn't the only reason I left Protestantism. There were several more. For example, almost all Christians follow the command Jesus gave at his Last Supper to consume bread and wine in remembrance of him (i.e., the Eucharist). However, most Protestants believe he was only speaking symbolically—that the bread and wine are just symbols that communicate an important truth about how

Jesus remains "spiritually" with us. The Catholic Church, on the other hand, holds that the bread and wine actually *become* the Body and Blood of Christ. Although they retain the appearance of bread and wine, Jesus becomes *really present* at the level of substance, essence, or reality.

This belief can be really difficult to grasp, and admittedly it took me a while. The Catholic view of the Eucharist depends on clunky philosophical terms. But for a simpler analogy, consider a bright star you see shining in the night sky. In reality, that star probably doesn't even exist. Due to the huge distances between Earth and the stars and the restricted speed of light, we see light rays from stars that have already burned out long ago. Thus the *reality* of that star's existence is different than its *appearance* to us. Similarly, Catholics maintain, even though the eucharistic bread and wine still look and taste like ordinary food and drink, their *reality* has shifted thanks to divine intervention. At the level of substance, they've really become the Body and Blood of Christ.

Now, this may seem like a minute theological difference between Catholics and Protestants. But it's actually quite significant. If the Catholics are right, then in every Catholic parish you can encounter Jesus in a real, physical, substantial way—not just spiritually in your heart. If true, this is beyond remarkable. But if Protestants are right, then what Catholics do at Mass—worshipping the transformed bread and wine—borders on idolatry. It involves worshipping mere food as if it were God.

So who is right? Is the Eucharist merely spiritual and symbolic, or do the bread and wine really become the Body and Blood of Christ?

Well, when researching this question, I was shocked to discover that the unanimous belief of the early Church, and the near-consensus view of Christians for fifteen hundred years, was the "real presence" view—in other words, the Catholic view. Every single theologian, saint, pastor, or preacher in the Church that I studied took the Catholic position. The Protestant view didn't arise until the Reformation, and only then, perhaps, because the Protestant Reformers sought to eliminate the Catholic priesthood. They figured if priests were necessary for Mass, and Mass was about this transformation of bread and wine, then the best way to get rid of priests was to get rid of the transformation. Hence, they shifted their view on the Eucharist, making it just a symbol; and priests, unnecessary.

Again, this is just one of several points in which I came to see the Catholic Church was true, and not just true but in continuity with the early Church and all ancient Christians.

That gets us most of the way but still not all the way. We may have eliminated some options, namely, those traditions that profess *sola scriptura* or "spiritual" communion, but what about the other options? Clearly Jesus didn't establish two, three, or four churches. He started one. So which church today has the best claim to be that same Church?

HOW DO WE FIND THE CHURCH JESUS ESTABLISHED?

The earliest Christians knew this was an important question. That's why, after much discussion and debate, they discerned four criteria to identify which church is the one Jesus established: the true Church must be one, holy, catholic, and apostolic. These four marks are included in the Nicene Creed, one of the oldest statements of Christian faith and one of the few creeds accepted by virtually all Christians—Catholic, Protestant, and Orthodox alike. Let's look at each of the marks.

First, the Church must be one. This means there must be unity in belief and worship. The true Church can't just be a collection of individuals, each believing and doing their own thing. Just as America would effectively dissolve if its citizens were free to accept or reject the Constitution or pick and choose which laws to obey, so the true Church must have a unified set of beliefs and practice. And the Catholic Church has this. While it is true that many self-identifying Catholics reject those beliefs, the beliefs themselves are nevertheless clear and unified. In fact, it's precisely because the Catholic Church has a coherent unity of belief that we can say this or that person diverges from official Church teaching. On the contrary, there is no unified "Evangelical" belief system or "nondenominational" belief system.

Second, the Church Jesus established must be holy. Please don't think that this means every Christian within it must necessarily be sinless. It doesn't mean that, and

Christians are the first to acknowledge what G. K. Chesterton expressed: "There are saints indeed in my religion: but a saint only means a man who really knows he is a sinner."[19] So what does this mean? It means two things. First, it means the source of this church, Jesus Christ, is holy. Second, it means the church must offer the means by which to tap into the holiness of Christ. Through its sacraments, that's precisely what the Catholic Church offers—proven routes to holiness—and their success can be seen through the remarkable holiness of its saints (we'll meet some of them later in the book).

Third, the true Church must be catholic. This doesn't mean the church identifies as the "Catholic Church," because of course any church could claim that title. By catholic this means the Church is universal or all-embracing. Is there a more all-embracing church than the Catholic Church, in this sense? No other religious tradition, much less Christian tradition, is so expansive, encompassing a larger range of countries, ethnicities, ages, classes, and temperaments. Other traditions, such as the Russian Orthodox Church, may be just as unified or holy, but they're not very catholic in this sense—they're generally limited to specific countries or ethnic groups. Yet James Joyce was right in *Finnegans Wake* when he described Catholicism this way: "Catholic means 'Here comes everybody.'"

Finally, the Church Jesus started must be apostolic. This is perhaps the most important criterion, especially when deciding between the Catholic Church and any number of Protestant communities. To be apostolic means the Church has a continuity with Jesus' first apostles and is able to trace its lineage directly back to them. The Catholic Church can do this. It has an unbroken lineage, stretching from the current pope to the pope before him and the pope before him, all the way through more than 260 popes and finally to St. Peter himself, the Church's first pope. When Jesus said he would build his Church on Peter, and when he gave Peter special authority to speak and teach in his name, he also imparted the ability to pass on that authority to others. (We can see why this was logically necessary; otherwise, when Peter died, the Church's divine authority would have disappeared with him.) Similarly, every Catholic bishop can trace his spiritual lineage in an unbroken succession of ordinations, all the way back to the apostles. Why does this matter? It ensures a spiritual continuity throughout time. It gives us a way to know whether someone has been commissioned to safeguard the Church's faith, taught and passed down by Jesus' original followers, or whether they stepped out of that line in order to start something new on their own. Unfortunately, that's precisely what has happened with nearly every Protestant church, the majority of which began just five hundred years ago (each was founded by a particular man who stepped outside of the apostolic line of succession). The Catholic Church is different. It claims to have divine roots. It is the rightful continuation of what Jesus started two thousand years ago. To be fair, it isn't the only church that claims this. The Eastern Orthodox churches claim something similar. However, those churches don't fulfill the other marks, or at least not as well as Catholicism.

Finally, besides bearing these four marks, the Catholic Church can also be shown true by examining the early Christian Church. What did it look like? How did it function? How was it ordered? I was surprised, as a Protestant, to discover how congruent the early Church was with the Catholic Church of today. It was arranged hierarchically, with bishops, priests, and deacons. They celebrated and prayed to saints. The focal point was union with Jesus Christ through the Mass, a religious service where bread and wine were transformed into Christ's Body and Blood. The early Church, through and through, was not only catholic—it was Catholic.

Whew! We've covered a lot in the first four chapters. We've seen good reasons to think God exists, that religion is good, that Christianity is true because Jesus is God, and finally that the Catholic Church offers the fullness of faith that Jesus inaugurated. Our goal was to show that Catholicism is true and that its truth is a very good reason to embrace it.

But that's not the only reason. Another reason to consider Catholicism is because it is good. When I explored the Catholic Church, I was obviously compelled by the Church's truth claims, but I was also impressed by its remarkable moral witness.

PART II

Catholicism Is Good

5

Because It Built Western Civilization

The great twentieth-century historian Hilaire Belloc wrote that "if the influence of the Church declines, civilization will decline with it. . . . Our civilization is as much a product of the Catholic Church as the vine is the product of a particular climate. Take the vine to another climate and it will die."[20] Is this just triumphalist exaggeration? Or is there something to Belloc's claim? Does Western civilization really depend on the Church?

Another historian, Thomas Woods, certainly thinks so. His bestselling book *How the Catholic Church Built Western Civilization* makes the case that the Catholic Church is responsible for much of our Western foundation. He writes, "The idea that the Church has been an obstacle to human progress has been elevated to the level of something everybody thinks he knows. But to the contrary, it is to the Catholic Church more than to any other institution that we owe so many of the treasures of Western civilization."[21]

Of course, most people recognize the Church's influence in music, art, and architecture. But the Church's contributions extend way beyond those fields. From science to law, economics, and morality, much of the cultural foundations we take for granted today are grounded in Catholicism.

Before getting to specific examples, let's be clear this doesn't mean Western civilization derives *entirely* from Catholicism. We can't deny the contributions of ancient Greece, Rome, or other groups. But the Church's contributions are massive, arguably more than any other source, and yet still go relatively unnoticed today.

During my own study of the Catholic Church, while weighing its pros and cons, these historical contributions were a major check in its favor. It was alluring to think I might hook onto an institution responsible for so many good things in the world, and not some historically irrelevant organization.

Let's look at just four of the many ways Catholicism has shaped our world: science, the university system, charities, and our system of law.

SCIENCE

Most of us swallowed a basic myth in school, namely, that while brave scientists were trying to uncover truths about the universe, bullying churchmen who hated reason and didn't want people to think for themselves did everything they could to stop scientific progress. Catholic philosopher Robert Sokolowski has argued that this is the founding myth of modernity, that our enlightened world was born out of, and in opposition to, prescientific religion.[22] (If you want proof of this theory, just glance at any Internet comment box, pop culture magazine, or late-night talk show—they're permeated by the view that science and religion are in conflict or they *were* in conflict but science long ago prevailed.)

The first problem with this view is that it paints with too broad a brush. Sure, *some* religions are in conflict with *some* scientific beliefs. But it's wildly irresponsible to deem all religions antiscientific. A second problem is that this view rarely includes specific examples: How specifically do faith and reason conflict? Which scientific experiment invalidated religion?

Thankfully, the myth is slowly fading away, at least among people who think seriously about this topic. Scholars, both religious and nonreligious, are increasingly noting the Church's contributions to science. They point first to the enormous pool of scientific influencers and innovators who were Catholic. That list includes lay scientists such as Louis Pasteur and Blaise Pascal. But it's also packed with Catholic clerics. For instance, Roger Bacon, a Franciscan friar, is credited with devising the scientific method. The first person to measure the rate of acceleration of a freely falling body was Fr. Giambattista Riccioli. The father of geology, Nicolas Steno, was also a Catholic father, a priest. Fr. Athanasius Kircher is held to be the father of Egyptology. Fr. Roger Boscovich is credited as being the father of modern atomic theory. The study of earthquakes was so dominated by Jesuits, a Catholic religious order, that seismic research became known as "the Jesuit science."[23] In fact, it was a Jesuit, Fr. J. B. Macelwane, who wrote the first seismology textbook in America in 1936.

The Church's scientific contributions are especially prominent in the field of astronomy. Most of us are familiar with Nicolaus Copernicus, who first showed the earth revolved around the sun. Yet few know he was a canon of a cathedral and likely *Father* Nicolaus Copernicus, a Catholic priest. He was but one of many pioneering Catholic astronomers. J. L. Heilbron, a leading scientific historian from the University of California at Berkeley, observes, "The Roman Catholic Church gave more financial aid and social support to the study of astronomy for over six centuries, from the recovery of ancient learning during the late Middle Ages into the Enlightenment, than any other, and probably, all other, institutions."[24] Even today, more than thirty-five craters on the moon are named for Jesuit scientists and mathematicians.

Maybe the Church's most interesting contribution is one that atheists often propose as a counter to religion: the big bang theory. In 1916, Albert Einstein first published his general theory of relativity, which confirmed the widely held view that the universe was eternally old and would go on forever, stable and unchanging. But then in 1927, a young Cambridge priest-scientist named Fr. Georges Lemaître came up with a new alternative. His calculations suggested the universe may actually be expanding, having originated from a single minuscule point. He called his theory "the hypothesis of the primeval atom," but it later became known, derogatorily, as the big bang theory.

Few people took notice of Lemaître's work. The same year he published his paper, he met at a conference Albert Einstein, who dismissed the young cleric saying, "Your calculations are correct, but your grasp of physics is abominable."

Then, in 1929, the scientific community was stunned by the findings of Edwin Hubble, whose cosmic observations confirmed Lemaître's thesis and effectively overturned Einstein's. It was one of the most revolutionary twists in the history of physics. In January 1933, both Einstein and Lemaître traveled to California for a series of seminars. After listening to Lemaître lay out his theory, Einstein stood up, applauded, and said, "This is the most beautiful and satisfactory explanation of creation to which I have ever listened."[25] To this day, Fr. Lemaître is considered the father of the big bang theory. (Notably, Lemaître was not jailed, condemned, or excommunicated by the Church. He was hailed by Pope Pius XI, both privately and publicly, and inducted into the Pontifical Academy of Science.) How many of us heard that story in high school physics?

I was blown away by all these contributions when I first discovered them. But even more than the number of Catholic scientists—*Wikipedia*'s entry for "List of Catholic scientists" includes more than 170 innovators—I was impressed by how the Church's theological beliefs allowed science to even get off the ground. Have you ever wondered why the scientific revolution happened where and when it did? Why didn't the early Greeks or the ancient Mayans or people from the Far East ever give rise to science the way it arose in the West a few hundred years ago? The answer, as one chemist put it in the title of her book, is that science was born of Christianity.[26] This isn't to say it was born of individual Christians, though you could make that case, as we saw above. It's to say that the very foundation of science stems from the Christian worldview.

Two things are required for science to commence.[27] First, people must believe the world is not divine. We take this for granted today, but many primitive cultures held that nature itself was divine and worthy of worship. For a vivid (fictional) example of this, see the film *Avatar*, in which the Na'vi people venerate nature and experience profound mystical connections to it. But if nature is divine, the very last thing you would do is experiment on it. You would never subject sacred elements to probing and evaluation. You don't analyze the divine; you worship it. And this was the view of almost every ancient culture—until, that is, Christianity came on the scene, by way of Judaism. The Judeo-Christian tradition proposed something radically new, that creation is not divine in itself but emanates from a divine Creator. It's a gift to be enjoyed and explored, not worshipped. This new revelation opened the door for science.

But the scientific revolution needed to crack the door a little further. Another requirement was that the world must be intelligible. Again, we take this for granted. We live in a world magnificently ordered, one following recognizable patterns. For example, consider the law of gravity. Every physical body in our universe is subject to the effects of gravity, and we can calculate and predict that effect to astonishing precision. But why does this law of gravity hold, everywhere and at every time? It certainly doesn't *have* to be that way. And why do we presume our calculations and predictions match reality? Why think, for instance, that our laws of mathematics actually describe the world as it really is? Why is it so rationally transparent? Statistically, as philosophers and cosmologists have affirmed, it would be far more likely that we would have lived in a whimsical world where things popped into and out of existence, without any consistent pattern, and that our laws of science and mathematics were completely out of sync with reality. So the fact that we live in a well-ordered, consistent world demands an explanation—and Christianity provides one. Christianity holds that the world was not random or disordered but was created by a supreme intellect—the *Logos*, to use the Greek word given in the Gospel of John—that imbues the world with its own order and intelligence.

Now we see why science arose from a distinctly Catholic Christian culture. It wasn't until Christianity had taken root and people felt free to experiment on an intelligent, well-ordered world that the scientific revolution began—and not just anywhere but in the Christian West. Catholic belief encouraged explanation of the natural world, since as Paul noted in Romans, God's invisible attributes such as his power and divinity can be known through his creation. Thus, for Catholics, each scientific discovery offered, in a sense, a glimpse of God.

Again, these accounts debunk the founding myth of modernity that science and religion conflict. Just the opposite is true. The Catholic Church's true role in the development of modern science is still one of the best-kept secrets of history.

UNIVERSITIES, CHARITIES, AND LAW

Yet science is far from the Church's only contribution to civilization. We can also point to the university system.

After the fall of Rome, the conquering barbarians had little interest in preserving education or ancient texts. So the Catholic monasteries stepped in. Devoted monks produced thousands of books and preserved many others. They established schools in their cathedrals and churches, creating an educational system that quite literally rebuilt Europe and that, a few centuries later, gave birth to the first universities complete with degrees and accreditation. One historian writes:

> The university was an utterly new phenomenon in European history. Nothing like it had existed in ancient Greece or Rome. The institution that we recognize today, with its faculties, courses of study, examinations and degrees, as well as the familiar distinction between undergraduate and graduate study, come to us directly from the medieval world.

> By the time of the Reformation, no secular
> government had chartered more universities
> than the [Catholic] Church. . . . Intellectual life
> was robust and debate was vigorous at these
> universities—the very opposite of the popular
> presumption.[28]

In addition to teaching people, the Catholic Church has also fed, healed, and housed more than any institution in history. It's hard to explain how rare this concern was in the ancient world. Charity was not praised as it is today. Certainly some ancient nobles helped finance public buildings or baths, yet most giving was self-interested. Donors often gave for the notoriety it earned them or because it put recipients in their debt. The idea that they should happily support the needy for their own sake, without reward or reciprocity, would have seemed absurd in the ancient world (with the minor exception of Jewish communities).

That's what made the Church's charity so revolutionary. Following Jesus' command to radically care for the poor and marginalized, Catholics were the first group to institutionalize charity for the poor, sick, widows, and orphans (again, excepting Judaism, from which Catholicism emerged). Early Christians imposed fasts on themselves so they could save the money they would otherwise spend on food and give it to those in need. They even cared for their enemies, serving prisoners and their own persecutors.

The individual examples are myriad. St. John Chrysostom founded a series of hospitals in Constantinople. St. Augustine established a hospice for pilgrims, ransomed slaves, and even gave away his own clothing to the poor. In fact, he reportedly told friends not to purchase expensive clothes for him since he would just sell them and give away the proceeds. Sts. Cyprian and Ephrem organized relief efforts during times of plague and famine. Even the notorious skeptic Voltaire later admitted that "perhaps there is nothing greater on earth" than the sacrificial care he encountered in Catholic hospitals.

We take it for granted today that charity is admirable and that we should give preference to the poor and forgotten. But these attitudes weren't mainstream until they arose through the Catholic Church.

Finally, besides science, universities, and formal charity, the Church laid the groundwork for our systems of law. In medieval Europe, law consisted mostly of custom and some statutory law. Yet as Catholics began to develop their own system of canon law, they would eventually provide the foundation for all of Western law. We can even trace the advent of international law to the Church. In the sixteenth century, in response to the horrific treatment of Native Americans, it was a Catholic priest, Fr. Francisco de Vitoria, who proposed new international regulations based on the biblical teaching that "all men are created equal," a line echoed in the United States' own Declaration of Independence.

Certainly no classical political philosopher would have accepted that all men are equal. Aristotle, Plato, and Cicero believed that certain elites, with elevated intellects and skills, were more worthy of respect and protection than lesser citizens. The idea that people are radically different in terms of intelligence, beauty, and virtue yet equal in dignity is a distinctly biblical conception, and it was Catholics who made it a convention.

To be sure, the Catholic Church has its blemishes. We shouldn't whitewash its history. One can readily point to corrupt clerics (even popes), the Church's somewhat violent past, and in the twentieth century, the horrific sexual abuse scandal. These are all indefensible—but they're also historical aberrations.

Although you may not find it celebrated in many textbooks, the Catholic Church has contributed a massive amount of good to Western civilization and has been, perhaps, its most indispensable builder.

Still, grand contributions are one thing, and they're beautiful in many ways. But during my own journey into the Church, I was equally impressed by the attractive witness of individual Catholics.

6

Because of Its
Heroic Charity

Before my conversion, I knew maybe a few well-known Catholics by reputation, such as St. Francis of Assisi and the pope. Yet I had no clue about the Church's long tradition of saints. When I discovered them, I became enraptured.

A wise friend noted that the right way to judge the Catholic Church is by its best members, not its worst. The Church is like a doctor who wants to heal sick people (Pope Francis famously called it a "field hospital"). Just as we wouldn't judge a doctor by the people who refused to take his medicine, and should instead consider the people who actually *took* his medicine to see if they were cured, so with the Catholic Church. We should examine the people who took *its* medicine, namely, the saints. These people were not only cured from diseases that affect the rest of us—selfishness, laziness, envy, and despair—but also became radiant models of virtue.

For instance, think of all the Catholic men and women who have willingly given their lives rather than denounce their faith. Is there a more impressive example of courage and conviction? Every one of Jesus' apostles, with the exception of St. John, died a martyr's death. Every single pope in the first century of the Church was killed for his faith. But perhaps that was just a short period of initial persecution, right? Think again. The twentieth century had more Christian martyrs than in all the previous centuries combined. That included the recently canonized St. José Sánchez del Río, the fourteen-year-old boy who stood up to corrupt Mexican authorities when they demanded he give up his faith. He refused. He was then tortured, mocked, and forced to walk to his own grave on lacerated feet. They gave him one more chance to deny his faith, standing on the edge of his grave. When he refused again, he was shot. His faith never wavered, and he died a hero.

To be sure, it's not only Catholicism that boasts heroically good men and women. There are plenty of upright atheists and agnostics, and other religious traditions have their own martyrs. But no tradition can match the varied and vast scope of Catholic saints. The saints of the Catholic Church are as inspiring as they are diverse. There's a saint for all seasons and all peoples.

Let's look at just three saintly examples, each of whom attracted me to the Church and who each reflect the goodness of Catholicism.

ST. LAWRENCE, THE MAN WHO DEFIED AN EMPEROR

The third-century Christians were well-acquainted with death. The Roman emperor at the time, Valerian, hated Christians, and he persecuted them relentlessly. His violence peaked in AD 258, when he commanded that all bishops, priests, and deacons be put to death. He also encouraged his guards to ransack their churches and confiscate all money and possessions.

The edict terrified Christians, the pope most of all. He knew if the emperor was targeting bishops and priests, his time was running short. So he decided to act. On August 4, 258, he ordained a young Spanish theologian, Lawrence, to become archdeacon of Rome. This gave Lawrence two responsibilities: to guard the riches of the Church and to deliver food and money to the poor.

The decision was made just in time. Just days after the appointment, Valerian captured the pope while he was celebrating Mass and beheaded him. Lawrence was next on Valerian's hit list and was captured, but before being killed, the emperor demanded that Lawrence turn over all the riches of the Church and gave him three days to round it up.

Lawrence moved swiftly. He immediately sold the Church's vessels and quietly dispersed the money to widows and the sick. He then distributed all the Church's property to the poor, without the emperor's notice.

When the deadline hit on the third day, the emperor summoned Lawrence to his palace and asked for the treasure. Lawrence showed no sign of worry. He entered the hall confidently and then, with great aplomb, gestured back to the door. It opened again, and streaming behind him poured crowds of poor people, all crippled, blind, or sick. "These are the true treasures of the Church," Lawrence said, enraging Valerian. One account even records Lawrence declaring, "The Church is truly rich, far richer than the emperor."

Predictably, Lawrence was immediately sentenced to death, only after being tortured on a hot rack, for which Lawrence had one final jest. While being roasted, he reportedly quipped, "I'm well done on this side. You might want to turn me over!"

Lawrence is but one of many Catholic saints who suffered and died for the sake of goodness. When you read accounts of the early Christian martyrs, you discover an endless stream of heroes, men and women who refused to capitulate to evil and would rather die than sacrifice their moral integrity.

ST. DAMIEN OF MOLOKAI, LOVER OF LEPERS

Another example of goodness is Jozef De Veuster, later known as St. Damien of Molokai. I first discovered him not through a book but through a picture, one I found shortly before I became Catholic. The photo was taken just before he died, and like a car crash, it was both revolting and fascinating. The man in the picture clearly looked close to death.

His puffy forehead sagged over his eyes and his cheeks appeared to be melting off his face. Yet what most captivated me was his single open eye, gazing out with a notable serenity. Who was this man? I thought. He didn't look defeated by his disease. He appeared poised and resolute, and as I came to know his life story, I discovered where that confidence came from.

In 1864, Br. Damien's brother, Br. Auguste, was scheduled to travel from Belgium to Honolulu as a Catholic missionary. But when Br. Auguste got sick, Br. Damien took his place. The somewhat naive twenty-four-year-old landed in Hawaii on March 19, 1864, and was shocked by what he saw. Hawaii was an island community beset by infections. Over the years, travelers and seamen had introduced diseases such as influenza and syphilis. Yet none were as bad as Hansen's disease, better known as leprosy. Leprosy devastated the people in many ways. The disease was untreatable, meaning people had no hope of recovery. This led most lepers into a deep depression. Also, leprosy cripples your pain receptors, which causes progressive degeneration of your skin, eyes, and limbs. Lepers became disfigured and eventually immobilized. Finally, since leprosy is extremely contagious, sufferers were isolated from their community and viewed as outcasts.

To curb the spread of the disease, Hawaiian authorities quarantined all lepers on the Hawaiian island of Molokai. Forgotten and underserved, the community became infected by every dysfunction—poverty, alcoholism, violence, and promiscuity.

The young Br. Damien saw all this when he landed at Molokai. But instead of fleeing, he told the local bishop he wanted to stay and serve as long as the Lord would allow. The surprised bishop introduced now Fr. Damien to the leper community, describing him as "one who will be a father to you and who loves you so much that he does not hesitate to become one of you, to live and die with you."[29]

Fr. Damien had no illusions about what his mission would entail. He knew working in the disease-ridden colony virtually guaranteed that he would become infected too. Yet he never wavered in his commitment. His superiors gave him strict advice: Do not touch them. Do not allow them to touch you. Do not eat with them. But Fr. Damien ignored the warnings. He committed to personally visiting every leper on the island to ask about their needs. He washed their bodies and bandaged their wounds. He tidied their rooms and did all he could to make them as comfortable as possible. He built coffins and dug graves, committing that each leper, even if marginalized throughout his life, would receive a decent burial upon death. This had a remarkably uplifting effect on the community.

What surprised the lepers most was that Fr. Damien touched them. Most other people were terrified of the lepers. In fact, one local doctor only changed bandages with his cane. But Fr. Damien touched the lepers, embraced them, and dined with them. As a priest, he traced his thumb on their forehead while anointing them, and he placed the Eucharist on their tongues. All of these actions spoke volumes to the dejected lepers. They showed that Fr. Damien didn't want to serve them from afar; he wanted to become one of them.

And after more than a decade of work, he finally did. The day that Fr. Damien feared arrived in December 1884. While soaking his feet in extremely hot water, Fr. Damien experienced no sensation of heat or pain—a telltale sign that he had contracted leprosy. The disease developed quickly, causing Fr. Damien to write to his bishop with the news:

> Its marks are seen on my left cheek and ear, and my eyebrows are beginning to fall. I shall soon be completely disfigured. I have no doubt whatever of the nature of my illness, but I am calm and resigned and very happy in the midst of my people. The good God knows what is best for my sanctification. I daily repeat from my heart, "Thy will be done."[30]

He also wrote home to his brother, saying, "I make myself a leper with the lepers to gain all to Jesus Christ."[31]

Even before contracting the disease, Fr. Damien spoke of himself and the people of Molokai together as "we lepers." He identified closely with those he came to serve and offered a powerful expression of solidarity.

Besides St. Damien, I discovered many other Catholics who have toiled among the poor and marginalized, pouring out their lives in service with little acclaim.

ST. TERESA OF CALCUTTA,
SERVANT OF THE POOR

Finally, we turn to the twentieth century—to recent memory. In the summer of 1948, a small Albanian nun, Sr. Teresa, spotted a woman lying in the road. She was half eaten by rats and ants, and looked almost dead. People passed by on either side, few taking notice of her, but the nun stopped. She carefully lifted the woman, cradling her like a precious work of art, and carried her to a nearby hospital. When the attendants saw the woman, they apologized and said there was nothing they could do; she was beyond saving. But Sr. Teresa wouldn't accept that. She refused to leave until they gave the woman a bed, and, after much bickering, the hospital staff finally relented. The obstinate nun got her way and helped the woman die with dignity.

Such was the start of the woman we now remember as St. Teresa of Calcutta, or Mother Teresa. In April 1948, Sr. Teresa decided to serve in the slums of Calcutta, where she first met the woman in the road and where she would eventually serve, feed, and care for thousands of others. She founded the Missionaries of Charity, whose purpose was to care for "the hungry, the naked, the homeless, the crippled, the blind, the lepers, all those people who feel unwanted, unloved, and uncared for throughout society."[32]

My friends who have visited Calcutta have struggled to describe how bad the conditions can be. "It's the worst part of the world, in almost every way imaginable," one friend told me. He described witnessing a level of poverty that was almost unfathomable, where people live on a handful of pennies a day, trying to scrape together enough food to survive just a few more hours. Clean water is little more than a rumor. Raw sewage flows through the streets and shanty towns, which are built with loose sticks and trash. Yet it's to this desolate hell on earth that Mother Teresa devoted almost her entire life.

That choice alone is heroic, but even more so when we discover what she did there. Her primary mission was to uplift people's dignity. People there thought of themselves as throwaways, the lowest of the low in Indian society. They lived in obscurity—nobody seemed to notice or care about them. They shuffled along, they got sick, and then they died just as quietly, many in the streets and gutters. Mother Teresa wanted to change this. She wanted people to know that they mattered and were valued. She, of course, nursed many of them back to full health, and distributed an extraordinary amount of food and water, but her primary mission was to uplift their dignity.

One story illustrates that goal. As her group of sisters expanded around the world, some of them discovered a poor man in Australia. He lived on a reservation but was completely ignored by everyone. The man never left his house, and when the sisters visited they found it shockingly dirty and disordered. When Mother Teresa was in town for a visit, they invited her to stop and see the man. When she did, she begged him, "Please let me clean your house. Let me wash your clothes and make your bed."

The man declined. But the nun persisted: "Please. You will be better if you allow me to do it."

After a little more pestering, the man relented. Mother Teresa cleaned his house and washed his clothes, and as she did, she discovered a beautiful lamp. It was covered with dust and looked as if it had not been lit for years.

"Don't you light that lamp?" she asked.

"Why would I?" he answered. "For whom? No one ever comes to my house. I spend days without ever seeing a human face. I have no need to light the lamp."

Mother Teresa replied, "Would you light it every night if my sisters came?"

"Of course," the man said.

From that day on, she ordered the sisters to visit him every day, and they did so without fail. Two years later, they received a letter from the lonely man, which he asked them to pass on to Mother Teresa. It said, "Tell my friend that the light she lit in my life still continues to shine."[33]

After reading countless beautiful stories such as that during my conversion, it was easy to conclude, That's the sort of religion I want to belong to. I didn't want to join a faith with merely nice people. If a religion was truly divine, if it was really being guided by the Son of God, then it must exhibit extraordinary goodness—and that's precisely what I saw in the Catholic Church. I didn't just see it in these individual saints either. I saw it in the Church's overall commitment to care and compassion. The Catholic Church serves more people than any institution in the world.

Not every individual Catholic is perfect—most obviously me—and the Church has its own share of missteps and problems, but I can't think of an organization that is more consistently and impressively good than the Catholic Church.

7

Because It Doesn't Go with the Times

When most people say they have problems with the Catholic Church, it isn't with the saints. They hear about people such as St. Lawrence, St. Damien, or St. Teresa and respond with admiration and enthusiasm. There is nothing wrong with *those* people. They're doing it right. It's everyone else that's wrong!

By that they often mean the institutional Catholic Church, specifically its rigid teachings—and even more specifically, those dealing with sexual or moral issues.

They wonder why the Catholic Church is so backward and oppressive. Why is it so rigid on everything from marriage to contraception, abortion, women priests, and homosexuality, even while other religious groups gladly modernize their views? Why can't the Catholic Church just tweak its views and get with the times? Catholicism would be so much more attractive if it were more flexible. (It's worth pausing to note how the push to modernize Catholic teachings usually only pertains to the realm of sexual morality. Few people demand the Church "update" its teachings on compassion for the poor, service to the sick, the value of peace, care for the environment, or its advocacy for the dignity of all.)

For the moment at least, let's bracket the assumption that modernizing religious teaching is a good thing. After all, it's not clear this *is* a good strategy for reviving people's faith and attracting new members (for counterevidence, just see the catastrophic decline among modernizing mainline American churches such as the Anglican Communion). Let's instead focus on the main question at hand: Why is the Church so inflexible with its teachings?

Many people see this rigidity as an obvious defect. To be inflexible means you're closed to new ideas and proposals, unwilling to breathe in the spirit of progress. In fact, it was one of the Catholic Church's own saints, Bl. John Henry Newman, who said, "To live is to change, and to be perfect is to have changed often."[34]

But it's important here to distinguish between *individual people* changing and changing *specific truths and teachings*. Of course, as Newman affirmed, each of us should undergo change and change often. Why? It is because we're imperfect creatures. We come up short in so many ways and can always improve.

But change is not a universal virtue. It's not good in all spheres of life. For example, we would never criticize mathematicians for being so rigid about the laws of geometry or the rules of multiplication. These teachings are emphatically rigid. Changing them would require not just audacity but also insanity. We all agree mathematical truths are objective; they're outside our control, true whether we like them or not, and therefore impervious to change.

On the other hand, there are many things we regularly do change. We're happy to update our speeding laws, musical preferences, and clothing styles. That's because these things are all subjective. They stem from human beings. They are formed, not discovered, and we can adjust them as needed. They're dependent wholly on human preference.

With that distinction in mind, we can then ask, which category do the Catholic Church's teachings fall into? Are they more like mathematical truths, objective and unchanging, or are they closer to speeding laws and personal preferences, subjective and always open to change?

The Church's answer is, both. Admittedly, *some* of its teachings belong to the latter category and could, in principle, be changed over time—think, for example, of avoiding meat on Fridays during Lent or the commitment to celibacy for priests. However, and here's the key point, the Church holds that many of its teachings have been divinely revealed, either directly by God or indirectly through the Bible and tradition. And in that case, the Church is only a messenger. It has no more authority to bend, change, or update those teachings than a mathematician has to adjust the Pythagorean theorem. It's a safeguarder of objective truths, not their innovator.

This realization was huge for me. When I first began seeing the Church as a protector and sharer of divine truths rather than an arbitrary rule maker, cooking up teachings and then declining to adjust them, my whole perception of Catholicism changed. I began to appreciate the Church for refusing to compromise its message, even before I believed that message was actually true. There was a certain virtue in the Church's rigidity: that even as the culture pounded on its doors and demanded the Church submit to its ideas, the Church, like St. Lawrence, refused to relent and instead carried forward its own God-given message. Call it inflexible or rigid, but I found it exciting and courageous. The Catholic Church, I discovered, was one of the few institutions that audaciously claimed to stand outside the stream of culture and live by another standard. It was, again, a rebel.

NOT A HUNDRED PEOPLE WHO HATE THE CATHOLIC CHURCH

This was part of the reason G. K. Chesterton became Catholic. He said the Catholic Church "is the only thing that frees a man from the degrading slavery of being a child of his age."[35] Most everyone else moves with the cultural current in whatever direction it flows. But Catholicism stands outside the flow. It makes no sense to accuse the Church of being on the wrong side of history, as despisers often do, for if what the Church says is true, then it was created by God and will last forever, and is thus beyond history.

Cultures come and go, rise and ebb. Today's fashions become tomorrow's castoffs. Those who marry the spirit of the age will find themselves widows in the next. So we should be wary of thinking that today's moral positions will always be in vogue. Certainly we've learned that lesson after witnessing slavery, apartheid, and the eugenics movement, not to mention twentieth-century communism.

But even supposing the Catholic Church has good reasons to be rigid, people still have difficulty with its teachings. They find some of them confusing and unlivable—I certainly did before becoming Catholic. Does the Church really expect people to not share any sexual activity before marriage? To remain married to the same person for life, even when feelings of love fade away? Can't women carry out the duties of priest as well as men, and can't same-sex couples love each other as much as anyone else? Why can't the Church just lighten the load for everyone?

Those are all good questions, and the Church doesn't discourage them. In fact, Catholics have thought long and hard about these issues and have written much about them. That's a great place to start. In fact, whenever I dialogue with Church critics, I patiently listen to their concerns but then like to ask whether they've read any of the Church's actual teachings, or defenses of those teachings, on the topics they struggle with. I'm surprised how many times I'm returned with a blank stare, as if that was a strange and novel proposal.

Many people criticize Catholicism without understanding the "why" behind its teaching—and sometimes not even the "what." Fulton Sheen, the great Catholic media evangelist of the twentieth century, had it right when he said, "There are not a hundred people in America who hate the Catholic Church. There are millions of people who hate

what they wrongly believe to be the Catholic Church—
which is, of course, quite a different thing."[36] During my
conversion, I found that many criticisms leveled against the
Church missed the mark, not because they were insubstan-
tial but because they were aiming at the wrong target. They
were either beating down a straw man or assailing the real
Church without allowing a moment for its defense.

Of course, we would never accept misinformed criticism
in regard to other serious questions. We wouldn't listen
to evolution deniers until they had at least read Darwin.
We wouldn't take anarchists seriously until they evinced a
thorough understanding of democracy. We wouldn't accept
NBA critics until they at least watched a few basketball
games and understood the rule book. A basic requirement
of criticism is that you first understand the other position,
grasping not only what it is but also why it is held. Ideally,
you'd also be familiar with the best defenses of that position—arguments that counter your own criticism. Until you
understand all of that, it's tough to fairly criticize any view
and show how it falls short.

LOVE AND THE PELVIC ISSUES

But let's get back to the particular criticisms. When most
people suggest the Church is behind the times, they generally have one of two things in mind: either its views on
sexual morality or what seems to be its repressive approach
toward women. So let's look at each one of those, beginning
with what journalist John Allen Jr. has termed the "pelvic

issues"—those revolving around homosexuality, abortion, contraception, divorce, and cohabitation.

A teacher at a Catholic university recently handed out notecards on the first day of class, asking her students to answer one question: What do Christians believe? A few of the answers, though not many, predictably mentioned God, Jesus, and salvation. But she was shocked that almost every single card referenced homosexuality or abortion (and many listed both). Most references were negative. One student responded, "I know Christians don't like gay people or women, but that's all I ever learned in Christian school. I don't know what else to list."[37] For many people, Catholicism is no longer a live option simply because they assume the Catholic Church condemns gay or divorced people. Since most of them have friends and family in those situations, they face a choice between the Catholic Church and those they love most. The loved ones predictably win.

But this is a false choice. There's nothing preventing Catholics from loving gay and divorced people, nor in suggesting that those people can live out fulfilling lives as Catholics and experience all the gifts God has for them in the Catholic Church. I wish we had enough space here for a thorough look at each of those issues—homosexuality, abortion, contraception, divorce, and cohabitation—but perhaps we can shine light on a few principles that bring clarity on the Church's position.

The first principle is that love is a gift. Love is not a tool or a selfish way to make us happy. Love exists for the sake of the other. In fact, love is, by definition, to will the good of another—to freely give up your own ego and desires in order to bring about someone else's good. This is why the purest and most admirable forms of love, the ones that bring tears to our eyes and tingling to our hearts, are examples such as the elderly husband giving every last ounce of his energy to care for his fading wife suffering from Alzheimer's; the bond between soldiers who vow to never leave each other behind; or the parent who sacrifices comfort and safety to protect a loved one (think the Harry Potter series, *Finding Nemo, Titanic,* and *The Road*). So that's the first principle, that love is a gift.

The second principle is that true love is always fruitful. It is the nature of love to overflow, to be life-giving, and to produce more than the sum of its parts. It's never closed in on itself, seeking its own interests. It always wants to expand and bear new fruit.

The third principle is that love is faithful. It's not temporary or valid only while expedient. It doesn't rise and fall with our emotions. It doesn't depend on conditions, such as, If you do XYZ, then I will love you in return. True love is unwavering and unconditional.

A final principle is that our sexual proclivities and experiences are not our main identities. Your sexuality doesn't define you; you're more than who you're attracted to or who you sleep with. This can be hard to hear, especially for modern ears. Our culture often says, You are what you do or, You are what you believe. But the Catholic Church doesn't buy that. It has a much higher view of humanity. It says, for instance, that persons struggling with alcohol are not, fundamentally, alcoholics. That may be a convenient label and worth using, but it's not who they are at their core. Likewise, the Catholic Church claims that the homosexual, the transgender person, and the divorcee are all more than whatever those labels suggest. Those are just surface-level descriptors. Our true identity lies deeper. At its core, our deepest identity is as children of God, everlasting splendors who radiate the divine life. That's your deepest identity; that's my identity. It's an indelible mark that can't be erased or usurped, no matter what we do or what we believe. Now, I understand this may sound like a sweeping claim, and we'll unpack it more in a future chapter, but for now, just consider this bold fact: you are not your sexual identity; your true identity is far more profound.

When we pull these four principles together, we begin to at least see the coherence of the Church's sexual teachings. Why does the Church prohibit divorce and remarriage? Love is resolutely faithful and marriage is "until death do us part." Marrying another person while our original spouse is still alive is an affront to love. Why does the Church say no to homosexual behavior? Is it because the Church is bigoted and hateful? No. It's because sex is the supreme act of love. It's about more than mutual pleasure and emotional union (although those are definitely crucial components). It's about the fruit of love that flows from the sexual act, namely, children (which is precisely why the government, like the Church, regulates sexual relationships but not other kinds of relationships—because sexual relationships tend to produce children). This is also why the Church prohibits contraception. Besides often degrading women into becoming objects for male pleasure, and correlating well with the rise of divorce, contraception severs the procreative dimension of sex from its unitive dimension. It communicates to your partner, I want to give you all of myself *except for* my procreative capacities. Those I hold back from you. Yet we all sense that love is a total expression, that true love requires a full offering of self. Anything less may be a good relationship, and it may be partly based on love, but it doesn't embody the fullness of self-giving love, the type of love that undergirds all good marriages.

Now, I can already sense objections bubbling up: Well, if the Church frowns on same-sex activity and contraception because they're not procreative, are you saying that sex is only valid if it produces a child? The answer is no. But all truly sexual acts, situated in the context of love, are at least open to the fruit of children, even if any particular act doesn't result in a child. (Similarly, all baseball teams are ordered to the act of winning a baseball game. Even if they go winless the entire season, they're still a real baseball team because they were ordered toward the right goal.)

You might also be wondering, Sure, these teachings look good on paper. They may be nice ideals. But you can't expect people to really meet them today, can you? Half of marriages end in divorce. The overwhelming majority of people use contraception. Gay and lesbian couples are on the rise. What do you say to all those people? I would say you were made for love—not a poor substitute or imitation of love but selfless, fruitful, total, faithful love that is always a self-gift.

Are the Church's moral teachings hard to accept? Absolutely. Are they countercultural? In almost every way. But what good thing worth pursuing isn't? What worthy goal doesn't require you to fight against our basest impulses and swim upstream? For what important goal are we not asked to rebel in some way?

Again, there's much more that can and should be said about these issues, but this is at least a start. The key takeaway is that the Church's teachings on the pelvic issues are not based on bigotry or whim but on love. There's coherence and compassion to these teachings; as for every issue, the Church asks, What are the demands of love? And it's this coherence and compassion that makes them good.

THE CHURCH AND WOMEN

Let's look briefly next at the role of women in the Church. Almost all Christian groups have flipped their views on women in recent years. It used to be that nearly all Christian leaders were male. That's no longer true. Thanks to the suffragist movement and the sexual revolution, first-wave and second-wave feminism, almost every denomination now welcomes female clergy. The Catholic Church seems to be the lone holdout, the only institution that stubbornly refuses to ordain women or permit contraception and abortion. How can we view its position as anything but anti-woman? How else would you describe an organization led exclusively by men who make across-the-board decisions about woman-related issues? Why can't Catholicism just get with the times?

This is a common objection, and like most objections, it's based at least partly in truth. At times, the Catholic Church *has* failed to appreciate what Pope John Paul II coined the "feminine genius." Even today, for example, Vatican offices continue to be led overwhelmingly by men, even though there is nothing prohibiting women from many of those roles. So there is legitimate reason for criticism.

But often what critics want is not more women administrators; they want women priests. That's really the issue. If women can preach as well, counsel as well, and serve the sacraments as well as men, why can't they be priests?

For a long time, that was my view too. The Protestant churches I grew up in, both Presbyterian and Methodist, had women ministers. And as a "spiritual not religious" young adult, I didn't see what the big deal was. Why was the Catholic Church so stubborn on this point? If they were having problems attracting new priests, why not allow women? The numbers would boom!

However, my problem was the one I hinted at earlier, namely, critiquing something I didn't even understand. If you asked me, "Why do you think the Church only allows male priests?" I would have shrugged and said, "Well, I don't know. That's the point! It's such a baseless teaching."

Yet it was my criticism that was baseless. When I eventually took time to study the Church's justification for this teaching, I was surprised. The Church bases it teaching primarily on the historical fact that Jesus chose only men for his apostles, his first priests. The Church believes he did this for a reason, that it wasn't arbitrary. Why did he do it? The Catholic priesthood is not just functional; it also has a symbolic dimension, one that requires men. When a man is ordained to be priest, he is commissioned to act *in persona Christi* (in the person of Christ) to his people. He represents Christ to them, especially during the Mass, the main worship service for Catholics. During his earthly life, Jesus often compared himself to a groom awaiting his bride, which is the people of God. And through the Mass Catholics enact this union, primarily through the Eucharist or "Communion" as it's sometimes known. To make that symbolic union effective, though, the priest must be male, representing Christ not just in his words and actions but also in his essential maleness.

That explains why Jesus chose male apostles. It wasn't because he was a male chauvinist (Jesus never sinned; also, all the evidence would argue otherwise on that one) or because he was bowing to the social conventions of his time (Jesus routinely broke the conventions). He did so because the maleness of priests mattered—and it still does. This isn't a knock against women. As one Catholic writer explains, "Reserving the priesthood to men is not a judgment on women's abilities or rights, any more than celibacy is a judgment on marriage, or marriage a judgment on single people. The teaching reflects the specific role of the priest in the Catholic understanding, which is to represent Jesus, to stand in his place."[38]

Again, as with the pelvic issues, there is much more to be said. We regrettably don't have space for an adequate discussion here. The point, though, is that while the rest of the Christian world has gladly capitulated to the demand for women priests, the Catholic Church has stood boldly and confidently, not because it is stubborn but because it has good reasons.

A REAL MESSENGER WITH A REAL MESSAGE

The Catholic Church makes a strange claim. It believes in divine revelation, which is to say it believes God has revealed to it special teachings and insights over the years. These have come in many forms. Sometimes God communicated through chosen leaders or prophets, such as Abraham, Isaac, Jacob, Moses, and Isaiah. He has also spoken through his own Son, Jesus of Nazareth, who walked the earth and interacted with hundreds of people (many of these conversations are recorded in the Bible). Yet he continues to speak through his Church, which Jesus described as his body and which he was commissioned to speak and act in the name of God.

This Church is the bearer of God's message, and that comes with a huge responsibility. As G. K. Chesterton observed, the Catholic Church is "the only thing that talks as if it were the truth; as if it were a real messenger refusing to tamper with a real message."[39]

This is why the Church stoutly refuses to change its teachings on morality or faith. It's not because it won't—it's because it can't. The Church is just the messenger, not the source. It's just the mail carrier, delivering someone else's letters. Indeed, if the Church had come up with all of its teachings on its own, without any divine inspiration or guidance, then of course it could just change any of them whenever it wanted, easily and often. But that's not what the Catholic Church claims to be.

I'll admit, it's tough wrapping your mind around some of the Church's teachings. But even if you can't quite do that yet, perhaps you can at least see the coherence behind them. In the Church's unwillingness to bend to cultural norms, perhaps you can at least appreciate its impressive moral integrity and courage.

Now, let's consider how those hard teachings are just one side of the coin. Coupled with the Church's extreme demands is the Church's extreme mercy.

8

Because It Offers True Forgiveness

Like many people growing up, I believed in God but didn't have a strong personal faith. I didn't pray much outside of church, except before mealtimes and in special emergencies. I never read the Bible on my own. I didn't know it was possible to have a relationship with God. For me, God was a loving, wise, but distant being—a sort of cosmic grandfather who was there when I needed him but otherwise remote.

Though I didn't know it at the time, I had embraced what sociologists call "moralistic therapeutic deism." It's today's most popular view of God. This view holds that God is concerned with two basic things: making sure we behave the right way (moralistic) and helping us feel better about ourselves (therapeutic). The last term, *deism*, adds that God does not personally interact with the world but only pops in on rare occasions, otherwise content with letting the universe run on its own.

In college, as I studied and learned more about God, I discovered two glaring problems with that view. First, it doesn't demand anything of us, and second, it offers nothing significant. For the moralistic therapeutic deist, God is just *there*, without consequence or reaction. And that sort of God didn't compel me at all.

It made me think: Where else would we celebrate such bland indifference? For example, imagine a baseball coach who was blithely ambivalent about his players, not caring what they did and not interested in personally interacting with them. Suppose at the beginning of practice he just said, "Ah, well, if you want to hold the bat like that, go for it, I guess. If you want to flail the ball underhanded, with your elbows flying all over the place, I don't mind. The most important thing is just to do whatever makes you happy. Just have a good time!" We would of course balk at such a coach. That might be an acceptable style when coaching four-year-olds (still, probably not), but no parent or player who actually loves baseball would accept it. Why? It demands nothing. It teaches nothing. It doesn't improve anything. It doesn't beckon the player to new heights. It doesn't call forth greatness or even exist in a world that suggests greatness is possible. It just accepts mediocrity with a wink and a smile.

People don't want mediocrity. All of us—you, me, everyone—want greatness; we want excellence. For evidence, ask yourself this question: Are you happy with where you are or do you wish you were better? I don't mean better in the sense of making more money, living somewhere else, or having more possessions. I mean, do you wish you were a better person? Are there virtues you wish you had or vices ·

you wish you didn't? When we're serious with ourselves, we know, deep down, the answer is yes. We know there's a mark to strive for, and we know we routinely miss it. Or as G. K. Chesterton put it, "We men and women are all in the same boat, upon a stormy sea."[40] Catholics have a word for this seasickness: sin. It's a spiritual disease and we're all infected.

Catholicism isn't the only religion that promises a cure. Almost every religion proposes an answer. In ancient times, some suggested we sacrifice animals to make up for our failures. Others claim the only escape is through moral effort, that we need to try harder and will ourselves to a better life. Some beat the disease by merely ignoring it or wishing it away, pretending that evil and sin are only illusions.

But Christianity offers a radically different answer. It says that the only way to become free of sin is not by doing something but by accepting something, namely, God's forgiveness, which was achieved through Jesus' death on the Cross. Jesus gave his life in exchange for ours, paying the price for our sin. The perfect man died to heal us of our sickness.

But how do we receive that forgiveness? Christians have different answers to this question. For most Protestant Christians, the answer is to pray to Jesus, privately with a sincere heart, and then he'll forgive you. And in theory, this sounds great. It means you can go to God alone, avoiding the embarrassment of admitting your sins to someone else. It's quick, easy, and painless to receive forgiveness.

But there are a couple problems with this solution. I recognized one of them while Protestant myself, namely, that it's easy to fool yourself into thinking you *aren't* really forgiven when you actually are or that you *are* forgiven when you actually aren't. In either case, you're left psycho-analyzing yourself, trying to determine whether you *really meant it* when you prayed for forgiveness or were just going through empty motions. It was nearly impossible to be sure you were forgiven, despite your best efforts. It all seemed to come down to feelings—*feeling* you're forgiven or *feeling* you weren't.

That leads to the second problem—a problem that Catholicism solves: it's not what Jesus prescribed. Jesus never suggested that people could accept his forgiveness through private prayers. Instead, he turned to his disciples, giving them authority to forgive sins in his name. He said to them, "Whose sins you forgive are forgiven them, and whose sins you retain are retained" (Jn 20:23). Obviously this would require people verbalizing their sins to the apostles or their emissaries. (Also, the apostles would need to hear the sins to determine whether to forgive them or not. In the Bible, we find that some sins are *not* forgivable, such as when a person shows no sorrow for his sins or is not willing to change his behavior. But again, the only way for an apostle to know this is to hear the sin and the person's reaction to it.)

To me, this all made sense. Through this practice we could *know* with objective certainty when we were forgiven because, after confessing our sins and expressing remorse, the apostle, who has God-given authority to forgive sins, could verify that the sin had indeed been forgiven—no feelings, no guessing, and no waffling back and forth. The sin was objectively gone.

Yet we're still left with a problem. If Jesus gave this authority to his original apostles, did that mean only *they* could forgive sins? In other words, after the last apostle died, the world would no longer receive forgiveness? That would seem odd. It would be somewhat merciless for God to abandon everyone else living after the first couple centuries. So that's why Jesus set up a Church, a divinely guided institution by which he could pass this authority through generations. When each apostle died, the Church selected a new successor to take his place. (We see this in the book of Acts, where Matthias replaces Judas, the disciple who betrayed Jesus.) The successor then received Jesus' authority through a special rite, in which other successors laid their hands on him, prayed to God, and thus made him a bishop, which is simply the title assigned to men chosen to be the apostle's successors. Finally, because each bishop is responsible for shepherding many Catholics—sometimes more than ten million per region—it would be impossible for him to hear the confessions of every Christian in his diocese and offer forgiveness—he'd be in the confessional 24/7! That's why each bishop ordains priests, groups of men who help facilitate his mission. The bishop authorizes his priests to participate in the ministry of reconciliation and forgive sins, which is what makes it practically possible for each Catholic to walk into any nearby parish, enter a confessional, speak to a priest, and walk out forgiven.

As it turns out, Jesus' way of forgiving sins is far better than the private prayer method I wrestled with as a Protestant. It brings objectivity to the equation and an assurance that you really are forgiven.

THE FONT OF FORGIVENESS

I remember the first time I went to confession. It was during my last semester in college, at the end of my long study of Catholicism. I felt drawn toward confession, even while it confused me. A few friends told me how refreshed they felt after sharing their sins with the priest, which struck me as odd. You want me to go into a dark room, tell a stranger my deepest faults and struggles, and then I'm supposed to leave feeling *better* than when I entered? Yes, they would say, that's exactly right.

So one afternoon, I summoned the courage and headed to a nearby parish. There was a line of people waiting inside, inching forward. Some people went in and out of the confessional quickly; others lingered for a while. When it was my turn, I still hadn't decided what to do. I knew a few sins for which I needed forgiveness, but I wasn't sure about others. Still, when it was my turn, I opened the confessional door and walked in.

The priest nicely welcomed me. I explained that it was my first time going to confession, but he said that wasn't a problem and that I shouldn't worry—he would walk me through everything. He first asked me to confess my sins, all that came to mind. At first this was hard and unnatural. But as each sin rolled from my mind to my tongue, I felt strangely lightened. The priest never displayed shock or repulsion. In fact, the whole time he kept his eyes shut and his head bowed down, deep in concentration. I never once felt as if he was judging me for my sins or measuring me up. I had the real sense that he was on my side, that as God's representative, he was praying alongside me for my forgiveness.

When I had finished my litany, he nodded his head and offered me a few words of counsel, including an act of penance (typically, this will be a prayer or some charitable work meant to counteract the sins just confessed). Finally, he invited me to offer an act of contrition. I didn't know what that meant, but he explained it was an expression of my sorrow for committing those sins and an intention, with God's help, not to commit them again. I later discovered this to be the element of confession most often misunderstood— or missed altogether. It's what keeps confession from being some magical Catholic get-out-of-jail-free card, as if Catholics could just sleep around or steal tons of money and then escape punishment by mumbling a few empty words to a priest. The act of contrition ensures that in order to be truly forgiven, you have to both be genuinely sorry for your sins and have a firm resolution not to commit them again. If you lack one or the other conviction, the sins remain unforgiven.

I awkwardly gave my own act of contrition and then the priest extended his hands over my head and spoke these words:

> God, the Father of mercies, through the death and resurrection of his Son, has reconciled the world to himself, and sent the Holy Spirit among us for the forgiveness of sins. Through the ministry of the Church may God give you pardon and peace, and I absolve you from your sins in the name of the Father, and of the Son, and of the Holy Spirit.

It's hard to express how liberating that felt. It was as if a large boulder I didn't even realize I was shouldering was lifted from my back. Sure, I had prayed many times before in private, asking God to forgive me for particular things. But there was always a haunting voice wondering, Are you *really* sorry for that sin? Do you *really* plan to change? You might *feel* forgiven, but are you actually? The Catholic practice of confession put all those questions to rest for me.

God gave his priests the remarkable authority to forgive sins in his name, offering penitents an objective way to know his forgiveness. Sometimes that experience is amplified by good feelings, as it was at my first confession. Other times it's not, as I later learned. Feelings of freedom and weightlessness can become dulled over time. Nevertheless, there's almost nothing that can match the comfort of knowing, objectively, that when you go to confession in good faith and hear the words of absolution from a priest, you're assured that your sins are wiped clean. You become a fresh slate, a new creation, freed from all that weighed you down.

EXTREME DEMAND, EXTREME MERCY

This is what warmed me up to the Church's admittedly strong moral demands. The Church's standards are high. Ask any person on the street about the goal of life and most will say, "To be a good person." But that's not enough for Catholics. Catholicism isn't out to just create good people, those who are morally mediocre. It aims to accomplish Jesus' own goal: for us to "be perfect, just as your heavenly Father is perfect" (Mt 5:48).

The Church wants perfection for us. This is why the Church refuses to say, "Well, as long as you're faithful to your wife *most* of the time, that's fine"; or, "It's okay to lie one or two times, just not *too* often." No, the Church demands we strive for the moral ideal, whether we attain it in this life or the next.

That may sound harsh and impossible, but that's precisely why confession is so needed. Coupled with these extreme moral demands is the Church's equally extreme mercy.[41] No matter how many times we miss the mark or come up short, the Church is ready to offer God's forgiveness and pick us up so we can try again. Consider this: any criminal, even the worst murderer, thief, or rapist, can walk into a confessional and, in an attitude of sincere repentance, confess serious sins. The priest will then offer counsel and perhaps assign a severe penance, but if he senses genuine sorrow and repentance, he will then say, "I absolve you from your sins in the name of the Father, and of the Son, and of the Holy Spirit." And that person's sins, before God, would be wiped away. Period. And if God can do that for them, why not you?

Stop for a moment and consider your own life. Have you done something bad, maybe years ago, that you still drag along? Something that still haunts you and makes you feel guilty? Maybe you betrayed a friend or spouse or hurt someone in serious ways. Perhaps you've lived selfishly or used people for your own gain. Whatever the case, the Church wants to free you from that guilt. It's the only place to find true and complete healing.

You can ignore your mistakes and pretend they never happened. But most of us have tried that. It doesn't work—at best it's a temporary strategy. No matter how much we repress our guilt, it always returns, stronger and more oppressive.

You might also try to just lower your moral standards and pretend the wrong things you've done weren't really so bad, that in the end you're basically a pretty good person. But this doesn't work in the long run either. What you need is to stop playing those games. You need the one real antidote to sin, the one way to vanquish your guilt, and the one chance to make amends and receive real and lasting forgiveness. You need the extreme mercy found in confession.

In the years since becoming Catholic, I've had the joy of seeing many people who stayed away from confession for decades return to the sacrament. One man hadn't been in over seventy years! Yet when they return, ask forgiveness for their sins, and hear the priest speak those words of mercy—"I absolve you from your sins"—they leave walking on clouds and often in tears. Their lives are never the same.

Whether you're not Catholic and have never been to confession or perhaps a former Catholic who hasn't been in years, stop searching for false solutions and find the objective relief that only this encounter can provide.

The Church is not an evil force out to condemn the world. It's a beacon of mercy, offering pardon and peace even to the worst failures among us. If that's not good, I don't know what is.

PART III

Catholicism Is Beautiful

9

Because It Cherishes Beauty

In his stirring novel *The Idiot*, Fyodor Dostoyevsky suggests that "beauty will save the world." Those words ring true for Catholics, and they've been cherished by Catholic priests, architects, musicians, photographers, and artists. Dorothy Day, cofounder of the Catholic Worker movement, took them as a personal motto, and they've been quoted in multiple Vatican documents, such as *The Via Pulchritudinis* (*The Way of Beauty*).

The Catholic Church holds that God is not just the fulfillment of truth and goodness. He is also supreme beauty itself, from which flows all the particular instances of beauty we experience in this world. This conviction is behind the Church's extraordinary commitment to beauty over the past two thousand years.

To be sure, it's an unusual commitment. Muslims prohibit any artistic rendering of God or the prophet Muhammad. While Judaism honors God with fine gold in synagogues, the faith doesn't generally place a strong emphasis on beautiful architecture, sculpture, or painting. Early Protestants (particularly Anabaptists and then Puritans) were suspicious of using beautiful things to proclaim God's truth, which led them to violently smash statues, altarpieces, stained glass windows, and other religious art. In fact, one leading Protestant reformer, John Calvin, not only preferred plain, barren worship settings but even banned the use of musical instruments![42]

The Catholic Church is different. It has never seen art as dangerous or debased—just the opposite. Art is valuable, first because the beauty of art points to the beauty of God, and second because creating art is a participation in God's very creative power. God is the supreme artist who fashioned the world, and each expression of art joins that masterwork.

Most of us are familiar with at least some of the Church's artistic heritage. Think of Michelangelo's Sistine Chapel or his *David* and *Pietà* sculptures. Or perhaps Raphael's Madonnas, Da Vinci's *Last Supper*, Dante's *Divine Comedy*, or the stunning Gothic cathedrals. (One art historian claimed, "The medieval cathedrals of Europe . . . are the greatest accomplishments of humanity in the whole theatre of art."[43]) But there's much more than just these famous works.

When I explored the Catholic Church, I stumbled across a document called *The Via Pulchritudinis*, put together by a Vatican department in 2006. It turned me on to this facet of the Church's life, this deep communion between the life of faith and the work of beauty. The document asks, "Is not the task of saving beauty that of saving man? [And] is this not the role of the Church?"[44] Yes to both, says the Church.

This yes was especially evident during the Italian Renaissance. In the late Middle Ages, as a new wave of artistic genius swept across Europe, it was the Catholic Church who offered the greatest support. Its financial contributions are well known. For instance, it was thanks to the patronage of Pope Julius II that Michelangelo, Raphael, and Donato Bramante (chief architect of St. Peter's Basilica) flourished.

Artists found even more support under Pope Leo X, whose court was the artistic hub of Rome. The pope joined together scholars, poets, artists, and musicians, and many of them even lived in the papal residences. Leo presided over magnificent banquets, dramatic or musical performances, poetical recitations, and exhibitions of art. According to atheist historian Will Durant, "It was without question the most refined court in the world at that time. . . . In mere quantity of culture, history had never seen its equal, not even in Periclean Athens or Augustan Rome."[45]

Catholicism was the fuel that energized the Renaissance. But it didn't just contribute religious subject. It also provided the rational framework that allowed the Renaissance to soar. Historian Thomas Woods observes that perhaps the distinguishing feature of Renaissance painting was linear perspective, which involved the depiction of three dimensions in a two-dimensional work. This technique required mathematical precision, based on Euclidean geometry, and a technique known as *chiaroscuro*, the subtle use of light and shadow. Both features existed in the art of classical antiquity, but they were relatively dormant until Western art revived them around 1300. Why did they suddenly reemerge at that time and place? Catholics had a distinct view of God as divine geometer, as one who ordered his creation with geometrical precision. Christians believed that when they studied and applied geometry, whether in mathematics or art, they were tapping into the same underlying structure of reality that God used in creation. This view bore tremendous fruit in the realm of Renaissance art.[46] In fact, this conviction, that geometric art offered a window into reality and ultimately into God, became the philosophical key that unlocked the Renaissance.

BEAUTY, A PATHWAY TO GOD

Yet despite its deep appreciation for art, the Catholic Church doesn't support art for its own sake simply because it finds art beautiful or inspiring. It's also because of how beauty lifts minds and hearts to God. Catholic philosopher Peter Kreeft noted this in a bestselling book explaining the Catholic faith. Kreeft included twenty rational proofs for the existence of God, ranging from complicated philosophical arguments to appeals to morality and religious experience. But the shortest and simplest was his "Argument from Aesthetic Experience." It reads like this:

> There is the music of Johann Sebastian Bach.
> Therefore there must be a God.
> You either see this one or you don't.[47]

He obviously meant this tongue in cheek, but like most good jests, there is some truth behind it. Many people have discovered God, or found the Church, *via pulchritudinis*, along the way of beauty.

Consider the great twentieth-century poet Paul Claudel. Brought up in a Catholic family, Claudel regularly attended church as a boy and made his First Communion at the age of eleven. But he later drifted away from faith, thanks to skeptical professors and neo-Kantian philosophy (which in his words "paralyzed the impulses of the heart").

By 1886, the eighteen-year-old Claudel was spiritually lost, a discontented drifter. But for some reason, on Christmas day, he was inspired to attend Mass at the Cathedral of Notre Dame in Paris. "It was the gloomiest winter day," he remembered, "and the darkest rainy afternoon over Paris."[48] His experience at Mass wasn't much different than the weather. He found the service dull and decided to leave. But then "having nothing better to do," he returned a few hours later for a prayer service.

Claudel listened to the psalms and prayers sung by the choir. The enchanting harmonies stirred something within him. While listening to the music, he walked over to a resplendent statue of Mary in the cathedral, and "then occurred the event which dominates my entire life."[49] The combined beauty of the music and statue evoked a sense of boundless innocence. He suddenly and profoundly understood that God was real. The experience was overwhelming. Tears and sobs racked his whole being as he felt a rushing sense of God's love pouring over him.

In an instant, my heart was touched and I
believed. I believed with such a strength of adher-
ence, with such an uplifting of my entire being,
with such powerful conviction, with such a certainty leaving no room for any kind of doubt, that
since then all the books, all the arguments, all the
incidents and accidents of a busy life have been
unable to shake my faith, nor indeed to affect it
in any way.[50]

Now, our inner skeptic might balk and think, Oh, come
on. Just hearing a song or seeing a statue made you believe
in God? How credulous can you be? But Claudel was no
simpleton. He was well schooled in literature and philosophy, a French poet and dramatist, and a diplomat who was
nominated for the Nobel Prize six different times. He wasn't
antirational—far from it. But in that moment at the cathedral, he experienced something that was, we might say,
suprarational, extending beyond the plane of mere arguments and reason. His brief encounter with beauty allowed
him a brief glimpse of a transcendent realm, a glimpse that
confirmed to him there must be something more to life than
what we experience with our normal senses.

At the end of the prayer service, Claudel left the cathedral warily. Walking home through the rainy streets, he felt
like a stranger in his own body. Later, he would often try to
relive the ecstatic experience of God's presence, but he never
could. The encounter was like a brief touch to an electrical

wire—momentary and shocking. It only happened once, but its mark affected his whole life.

THE OPEN SEA OF THE BEAUTIFUL

That's the power of beauty, and it highlights why the Church cares so much about it. Few of us have experienced beauty in such a dramatic way as did Claudel, but we have experienced it. Perhaps we were captured by a moment in nature, gazing across a royal mountain or expansive valley, or maybe while pondering the wild colors of a sunset. Perhaps we've been stunned by a beautiful song, a beguiling painting, or a profound movie. Or perhaps we stepped into a breathtaking cathedral with beams and buttresses soaring into the sky, lifting our soul with them.

The pattern is always similar. We encounter something beautiful and then fall into aesthetic arrest—we're stopped in our tracks and inspired to contemplate what we see or hear. In that moment we feel a tinge of the numinous. It's as if we're briefly in touch with another realm, as if something reaches out from beyond and tugs on the strings of our heart. Finally, if we force ourselves to push forward, we wonder about the source of all beauty: Where does beauty come from? Why does it have this effect on us? And how can we drink in more of it? Plato, in his *Symposium*, suggested that from one particular beautiful object, we can finally rise by a steady process to "the open sea" of the beautiful itself.[51]

Through this process, we're led to realize there is something *more* to reality than the material world. That's a radical idea today, as most people—especially young people—have become comfortable with a flattened-out, secular realm in which the only real things are those proved by science. The Catholic Church rejects that and points among other things to beauty; science can't explain beauty, much less its source, Plato's "open sea" of the beautiful. For instance, when we're enraptured by a painting, we just know, with strong conviction, that it's something more than mere atoms on a page, that even a complete scientific analysis will not tell us everything worth knowing about it. Similarly, we know that a sunset is more than just chemical reactions in the sky, or that a beautiful symphony is more than just vibrating sound waves in metal tubes. Beauty is a signpost to what lies beyond—it points somewhere else, ultimately to God.

And that's why the Church has safeguarded and promoted beauty for two thousand years. It's a beautiful religion. When I was in college, trying to decide which religion, if any, to follow, I knew the answer had to be one that was not just true and good but also beautiful. That's what I found in Catholicism.

To be fair, it's worth admitting that while the Church, in general, has championed beauty in every century, there are gaps. Indeed, the average day-to-day experience of many Catholics today—myself included—is probably a far cry from the aesthetic arrest Claudel experienced in Notre Dame. To be frank, many modern Catholic buildings are simply ugly. But it's the Church's very emphasis on beauty that allows us to see this defect, to recognize bland, functional buildings, banal music, or cheesy art as real failures, as bugs in the system. They're lapses, symptoms of aesthetic amnesia. Dostoyevsky had it right: the world is sick and starving for wonder. And beauty is the cure. That's what the Church offers: the medicine of beauty.

I could never have joined a Church that thought beauty was insignificant, bearing no connection to a higher world (much less one that banned music, icons, or stained glass windows!). Thankfully, I found a Church that taught just the opposite. Catholicism cherishes beauty and champions the arts because both lift up the soul of humanity.

Yet that's not the only way Catholicism raises us up.

10

Because It Lifts Us Up

There are all sorts of skeptics. You have the materialists, those who only believe in the physical world—no souls, no God, and no angels. You have the free thinkers, who reject any dogmas and intellectual constraints (at least ostensibly). You have the rationalists, who pride themselves on clear and critical thinking. And, of course, you have the atheists and agnostics, those who don't believe in God and those who aren't sure.

Each of these labels highlights one facet of skepticism, and each, at least etymologically, makes sense. For instance, "materialist" is a good descriptor for someone who only accepts material reality; "atheist" (in ancient Greek, a = without; *theos* = God) is appropriate for someone who rejects theism.

But one label has always bothered me, one that just doesn't seem to fit its definition. I saw it pop up in college, when a student group chose it for their name, and even then it struck me as off base. That label was "humanist."

Humanism stems from the Enlightenment, and the term is meant to elevate humanity's role in the world. Its adherents believe "man is the measure," as the saying goes, that humans are responsible for giving life shape and meaning. Humanists typically move the spotlight away from God and instead shine it on humanity. If history were a play, humanists see humanity as producer, director, and most importantly, star. There is nobody else behind the curtain.

And to give credit where due, there is some partial truth to humanism. From art to architecture, poetry to politics, planes to computers, and science to medicine, the human story *is* remarkable and breathtaking. Humanity is truly great and is responsible for so much good.

The problem is the next step, the humanist conclusion that affirming humanity's great role requires denouncing God. They see humanity as locked with God in a zero-sum struggle, as if we could only elevate one or the other. Either humanity or God, but not both, can be responsible for human success. Either humanity or God, but not both, is pulling the strings.

And if humanists see God as humanity's great enemy, the Catholic Church isn't far behind. Catholicism is usually depicted as the most antihumanist faith around, a system marked by an array of controlling laws that thwart humanity's freedom and self-expression, especially in the realm of sexuality.

And that was what I thought about it too—until I actually explored Catholicism. When I did, I found something remarkably different. The Catholic Church indeed emphasizes the providence of God, affirming that everything in the cosmos falls under his control. But at the same time, it also exuberantly teaches that humanity is responsible for so much human progress.

This apparent paradox is perhaps best summed up in the words of the biblical prophet Isaiah: "Lord, you will decree peace for us, for *you* have accomplished all *we* have done" (Is 26:12, emphasis mine). How can that be? *You* have accomplished all *we* have done? Isn't it either/or? Either humanity is responsible or God is responsible, but not both, right?

The Catholic Church offers a third option, and it's evident in Isaiah's line: God and human beings are not at odds and are not competing in some cosmic struggle for power. Instead, God and men cooperate in harmony, toward the same end, much as the winds and brass in a symphony join together without conflict.

Once again, this was a fascinating discovery for me. It called to mind a youth basketball team I was coaching at the time in college. The team was full of hyper six- and seven-year-olds, and at the first practice it was clear the kids knew virtually nothing about basketball. Worse, they showed no interest in learning. I spent most of our practice time trying to wrangle them in place and keep them from throwing balls at each other. But after a few practices, they eventually settled down. We started running drills. I taught them the proper ways to pass, shoot, and dribble. By the time our first game rolled around, the improvement was monumental. I was thrilled to see them dribbling and making good passes; they even made a few baskets! I felt I had accomplished something real and genuine through them.

Now, think back to Isaiah's line: "For *you* have accomplished all *we* have done." In a way, my team could have said the same thing about me after that first good game. Of course it was *them* dribbling the ball, *them* making sharp passes, and *them* scoring baskets. But they couldn't have done it without me. In one sense, *they* were responsible, but in another sense, it was *I* who accomplished all of that through them.

That's not a perfect analogy, but it illustrated a crucial principle for me that uncovered a new facet of the Church's beauty. Catholicism teaches that God delights in working *through* secondary causes, including and especially humans. He doesn't see us in opposition to himself, as ancient Greek and Roman deities did. We're not in some grand tussle with the gods, who are out to dominate and manipulate us. We cooperate with God to bring about his purposes, and in so doing we participate in his life—we taste divinity.

So that all summarized one problem I had with humanism. Humanism presumes that lifting up humanity means putting down God, when in truth we can celebrate the harmonious work of both.

A second problem I encountered was perhaps more significant. I came to see that humanists not only underestimate God's contributions but also underestimate *humanity's* dignity and capacity. In truth, it's Catholicism that takes the highest view of humanity—even higher than does humanism. Or as Bishop Robert Barron puts it, more provocatively, "Catholicism offers the greatest humanism possible."

How can Catholics make that claim? The answer lies at the beginning.

IMAGO DEI

The first book of the Bible, Genesis, proffers the story of how our world began, including massively important truths about humans and their purpose.

It's worth pausing here to deal with a common hang-up. Many non-Catholics presume that Catholics, like some but not all Protestant Christians, read the book of Genesis literally, as if God created the world during a literal seven-day period or literally put his mouth to the nostrils of primordial man and breathed life into him. But most Catholics don't read Genesis that way. They read it as poetic narrative, a figurative account of nevertheless real events. The author of Genesis employs mythic language to answer big metaphysical questions such as why the world was created, where humans come from, and what their purpose is. It is simply not interested in reporting scientific facts, such as details about big bang cosmology, the age of the universe, or whether God employed evolution during the creation process. (We know the Bible isn't teaching science, especially since the whole enterprise of science would not emerge until centuries later.) So it's important we don't fall into that trap.

But getting back to the narrative, of all the truths Genesis unveils, perhaps the most startling is this one: humans were made in the *imago Dei*, the image of God. After creating stars, oceans, plants, and animals, God takes stock of everything and calls it good, and yet something is still missing. Therefore, he decides to create one more thing. He says, "Let us make human beings in our image, after our likeness" (Gn 1:26).

What does this strange description mean? How are humans created in God's image? The earliest Christians pointed to three abilities that humans alone share with God: reason, free will, and love. Unlike any other creature, humans have a rational mind. We can consciously reflect on the world, even on ourselves. We also have free will. We're the only creatures that can transcend mere instinct or bodily desire, freely choosing to behave one way or another or choosing between two courses of life. Finally, we are the only creatures capable of love, of an altruistic act of self-gift to another.

Of course, for humanists, this Genesis account could hardly be more wrong. They believe there is no substantial difference between humans and other creatures. Humanity evolved more rapidly and effectively than other species, but given enough time, other creatures could perhaps develop the same capacities as humans. In other words, humans only differ in degree, not in kind.

But Catholicism holds that humans *are* radically different than other creatures, and not just because they're smarter or more creative. It's because they bear the likeness of God. They have been, in a sense, divinized, marked with a transcendent dignity.

DOES IT REALLY LIFT UP ALL PEOPLE?

But if that's the case, you might be thinking, why does it seem as if the Catholic Church steps on the dignity of so many groups? Sure, Catholicism talks a good game about lifting us up and respecting the dignity of all. But aren't there groups it *doesn't* lift up? What about homosexual men and women? Doesn't the Catholic Church condemn them? How can anyone say Catholicism lifts up people when it rejects so many lifestyles?

These are all good questions and worth addressing. I asked them myself when exploring Catholicism, and the answers I found were not what I expected. Two principles emerged during my study. First, the Catholic Church is committed to the dignity of all people, without condition. Even as a non-Catholic, I could appreciate this. The Catholic Church seemed to value human life across its full spectrum. I noted how it led the way in protecting the dignity of unborn children, the uneducated, the poor, the sick, the homeless, the elderly, and the dying. As noted earlier, no other group feeds more people, heals more people, teaches more people, or houses more people around the world. That led me to ask, why does the Catholic Church do all this? The answer, I discovered, is that the Catholic Church is convinced every person was created in the image and likeness of God and thus bears an innate dignity. That dignity does not come from what people do or how useful they are. Nobody can increase or decrease someone's human dignity.

That dignity is always there, even when others ignore it. It's an unwavering fact because of *who people are* as children of God, not because of how they perform or what they contribute to society.

It's easy to take this fact for granted. But we should pause and note how unique this view is. Most of society holds, if only implicitly, that our value hinges on some condition—it's relative. Your worth depends on what you contribute, what you accomplish, how big your bank account is, how many resources you consume, whether your lifestyle is socially acceptable, and how much power or privilege you have. But the Catholic Church says no to all of this. Every life is equal in dignity, and every life is worth protecting and honoring because it carries an inviolable, God-given dignity—no qualifications.

Why is this first principle so important? It grounds the second important principle, that the Catholic Church is the greatest friend of marginalized men and women—including the poor, sick, elderly, and yes, even homosexuals. Now, I know that's a bold and provocative claim—especially the last part. But it's true because of the Church's unrivaled conviction that all people, regardless of sexual orientation, have inviolable dignity worth defending.

Modern society has not always embraced this view. Historically, any time cultures began seeing dignity as something malleable or earned, the first casualties were those on the margins, those not loud or powerful enough to champion their own worth. In the past, this too often included homosexual men and women. We're quick to forget this since our culture is generally positive toward homosexual lifestyles. But that could change, as it has many times throughout history—for example, all you have to do is look to recent regimes in Germany, Russia, Cambodia, and throughout many parts of Africa. Catholic philosopher Peter Kreeft explains this principle further:

> One of the things I fear from [social relativism] is an ugly backlash against homosexuals. If the truth is now whatever we will, then just as there is nothing to stop society today from redefining marriage, there is nothing to stop it tomorrow from redefining personal dignity and rights so as to take them away from homosexuals. The Nazis did exactly that.
>
> The Church is the best friend of homosexuals, both because she tells them they are made in God's image and have intrinsic dignity and rights and are called to be saints, and because she is the only social force left that insists on moral absolutes—so when they sin against themselves she says NO, just as she does to heterosexuals who sin against themselves sexually. But when others sin against homosexuals she says NO also.
>
> No one else dares to say NO. The Catholic Church speaks up for everyone, including homosexuals.[52]

Again, I know this probably sounds startling and countercultural—it did to me when I first considered it. But that's because it is. It's precisely that. It's exactly counter to the way our culture views human dignity, sexuality, and behavior. The culture shouts, "I am my behavior! If you don't approve of my sexual choices, you must hate me!" But the Church quietly and patiently responds, "No, my child. You are far more than your behavior or your sexual choices. You were created in the image of God. You have inestimable worth and a divine destiny. And I will never stop fighting to protect that worth, no matter how you behave, what you choose, or who you are."

ETERNAL GLORY

Catholicism is ultimately the greatest humanism because it lifts up humanity, not just to great earthly heights but also to the very doors of heaven. This point was forcefully made to Bishop Barron on a retreat he recently attended. One of the other attendees was Fr. Godfrey Diekmann, a leading Catholic theologian. Diekmann was by then in his upper eighties, but his mind, wit, and tongue were still as sharp as ever.

As Barron sat and listened to Diekmann's stories, he was inspired to ask, "Godfrey, if you were young again and you could mount the barricades, what would you speak out for today in the Church?" The old man hit Barron on the knee with his cane and said without hesitation, "Deification."

He was referring to maybe the most astonishing Catholic doctrine: God became human so that humans might become God. Catholicism teaches that we human beings are, in Christ, being transfigured into divinity. We were made not just to love and worship God but also in some mystical way to participate in his very life.

As I discovered, this serves as one of the few master ideas around which all other Catholic teachings revolve. I spotted it almost everywhere in Catholic tradition, across the writings of the early Church Fathers, in the soul-lifting art of its cathedrals, in the resplendent beauty of its liturgies, and in the rising harmony of its music; all of it seemed to be pointing to this key fact that humans were made to ascend, and not just high but all the way up into the very life of God. No other faith, whether Protestant, Muslim, or Buddhist, proclaimed such a glorious destiny, at least as fully or beautifully.

But lest we be confused, it's important to clarify that the Catholic Church doesn't teach that we *become* God, as if we will somehow replace him or become like Hercules, part man and part God. That's not what it means. Bishop Barron clarifies:

> At the center of Christian faith is the dizzying truth that God has broken open his own heart in order to allow us to share his life. The Father sent the Son into godforsakenness, into marginalization, physical suffering, psychological agony, even into death itself, and then in the Spirit he called him back. But in the return to the Father, the Son carried with him all of us whom he had embraced, showing us that nothing can finally separate us from the heartbroken love of God. When we, through Baptism, enter into the drama

of Christ's mission, we are deified, made children of God, rendered holy. The holy life is not primarily about moral excellence or spiritual athleticism or any sort of human achievement; it is about being drawn, by grace, into a dignity infinitely beyond our merits or expectations. Diekmann was right: It is about deification.[53]

The Catholic Church holds out this awe-inspiring destiny of humanity not just to a small group of the spiritual elite but to *everyone*. This brings us to one last beautiful fact about the Catholic Church.

11

Because It's for Everybody

Antarctica is not just cold. It's almost unfathomably frigid. With winter temperatures dipping below –100 degrees Fahrenheit, it's tough to imagine anyone living there. Yet people do, and they aren't just crazy thrill seekers. A rotating group of scientists and government officials carry out their work on the frozen continent. And like any other people, they have spiritual needs.

So the Catholic Church stepped in and did what it does best: it built a church—but not just any church. The chapel at the Belgrano Base in Antarctica is an ice church. It looks like something straight out of Hoth or Arendelle. Its walls are carved completely out of ice. Deep beneath the arctic surface, the church stretches through long frozen tunnels with crucifixes hanging along the ice-sheet walls. A simple altar sits at the front with only four chairs in front of it—a small congregation, but still, there it is! A frozen church, hidden underneath the coldest place on earth.

This highlights a fact that struck me early and often about Catholicism. No matter where you go, no matter what country you're in or what language is spoken, somewhere nearby you'll find a Catholic church. In many ways, Catholicism is the most universal religion. It's in the most countries and celebrated by the largest diversity of cultures. It's not constrained to just one part of the world or one ethnicity, as with some faiths. It stretches through South America, Latin America, and the United States; it's booming in Africa and Asia; and it's, of course, rooted in the Middle East (where Jesus was born, lived, died, rose again, and ascended into heaven) and Europe. It's truly a religion for everybody, everywhere.

Catholicism is capacious; it's roomy. Regardless of your background or interests, your political or social persuasion, or whatever makes you tick, you'll find a comfy section of the Catholic Church in which to feel at home. That diversity is beautiful. It's like a tapestry with many colors.

When I explored other faiths, including most Protestant traditions, I found them fairly monochromatic in comparison. They were typically isolated in one place or subculture, or they had one distinctive character. But when I looked at Catholicism, I found a faith with something for everyone, holding many different people and perspectives together. For instance, the Catholic Church includes prayerful monks who never leave their monasteries and social justice warriors who are constantly in the streets. It welcomes the introverts who pray and work alone and the extroverts who live in vibrant communities. It includes the wild tribal liturgies of Africa with dancing and loud music as well as the subdued formal liturgies celebrated with solemnity in Latin. It's open to super-smart scientists and plain-minded peasants. You find all types of people, vastly different and anything but monotonous, all linked together in the Catholic Church.

This is worth emphasizing because not a few people have had one bad experience of Catholicism, or have only seen one side of the Church, and think the whole thing must be that way. They think, Well, if the Catholic Church is like *that*, then it's not for me. But during my conversion I found that there's almost always another side, another facet, to explore.

To emphasize how welcoming and diverse the Church is, let's look at a few different types of people for whom the Church provides a home.

THE THINKER

I kept hearing the name: Thomas Aquinas. Bloggers and writers mentioned him with almost hushed reverence. They reverenced him as Hogwarts students did Dumbledore. Like the wizarding headmaster, Aquinas was renowned for his extraordinary wisdom, virtue, and good sense.

I naturally wanted to learn more about him so I opened Amazon.com and ordered his masterwork, the *Summa Theologiae*, or at least *part* of his masterwork. I bought just one volume of the *Summa*. The full text stretches over 1.5 million words and fills 2,565 pages in its most popular, English-language edition. The sheer size of the books is intimidating, and it doesn't get less daunting when you open them. I was bowled over by the *Summa*'s complex metaphysics and theology. To be honest, the first time I read Aquinas, I found him blindingly difficult. Reading him was like trying to stare at the sun. Of course, I didn't feel any better when I discovered, in his introduction, that Aquinas intended the *Summa* as a primer "to instruct beginners" (thanks for the ego boost, Thomas).

Thankfully, I had enough sense to realize the problem was with me, not him, that I just wasn't ready yet to tackle such a difficult text. It took a few years, and much more study, before I returned to the *Summa*. I read many books on philosophy and theology in between, which familiarized me with Aquinas's terms and arguments. As a result, my second encounter with the *Summa* was a totally different experience. I was mesmerized. Truth seemed to radiate from each sentence. Even though I knew I was still grasping just a fraction of what Aquinas was saying, I knew I was dealing with one of the greatest, most brilliant minds Western culture had ever produced.

Whatever he touched upon—faith, social questions, morality, Jesus, or the Church—he deftly handled the topic with the precision of a skilled surgeon. It wasn't just his answers that impressed me. I was just as enthralled by his method, known as the *quaestio disputata* (disputed question). On each page of his *Summa*, Aquinas considers a pressing question—more than 2,600 in total. But before offering his answer to the question, he poses a few of the best counter-responses. Aquinas forms these objections to his own position so well that they're often more powerfully stated than his opponents' versions (for instance, see his strong but succinct objections to the existence of God). Then, and only then, after he puts forward the best case *against* his own position, does he carefully refute the objections and offer his own view. The result is impressive. Seeing him fairly present both sides of a question, and then masterfully defend his position, leaves you thinking, Here is a real genius at work, someone whose mind sees the whole picture.

Perhaps you're drawn to the life of the mind. If so, you'll be glad to discover not only Aquinas but also an entire patrimony of world-class intellects and scholarship in the Catholic Church. You see this in its great scholars and saints, and even in its seminaries. While most Protestant faiths require ministers to study for three or four years before leading a community, Catholic priests undergo a rigorous eight-year formation process leading to advanced degrees in both philosophy and theology. This is just one example that has convinced me Catholicism is the world's *smartest* religious tradition.

Now, does that make it true? Of course not. Perhaps all the Catholic Church's geniuses such as Aquinas and Augustine, Anselm and Pascal, and Newman and Edith Stein were right about everything *except* their religion, the thing they cherished most. I think that's a long shot, but even were that true, I challenge anyone to put forward a religious tradition that has more seriously wrestled with the biggest questions of life, from God to morality, evil, and even to existence itself.

The Catholic Church will never require you to check your mind at the door. In fact, just the opposite: it demands you *use* your reason to love God with not only all your soul and strength but also all your *mind*. And its impressive intellectual tradition has celebrated those who have done just that.

THE PARTIER

G. K. Chesterton once wrote that "in Catholicism, the pint, the pipe, and the Cross can all fit together." And he would know. Before and after he entered the Catholic Church, Chesterton was often found with a mug in his hand and a pipe in his mouth at one of the pubs dotting Fleet Street in London. He imbibed with not just other Catholics but even intellectual opponents, such as the atheist George Bernard Shaw. Chesterton's faith was jolly and welcoming, and its rollicking flavor was shared by his close friend, the historian Hilaire Belloc. It was Belloc who wrote the famous "Heroic Poem in Praise of Wine" as well as this quatrain, which he's probably best remembered for:

> Wherever the Catholic sun doth shine
> There's always laughter and good red wine.
> At least I've always found it so,
> *Benedicamus Domino!*

During their many hours around the pub table, Chesterton and Belloc liked to invent drinking songs. Some even dealt with their faith, such as Belloc's "Song of the

Pelagian Heresy." This bubbly belief led the sci-fi writer H. G. Wells to quip that "Belloc and Chesterton have surrounded Catholicism with a kind of boozy halo."

Some people think Catholicism is something sad and sullen. But just look at these two Catholic men and you'll find something different. It was their faith that led them to party. It was because they understood that life is a supreme gift from a divine giver that they believed every day, and every experience, was worth celebrating. For Chesterton, the central claim of Catholicism, that God became man through the Incarnation, in a way sanctified all ordinary human activities—including and especially drinking with friends in a pub. Even that experience could offer a foretaste of heaven.

To be sure, this doesn't mean all Catholics love alcohol or partying. While the Church uses wine in every Mass, it also has a long tradition of abstinence, both periodic and permanent. I'm not suggesting that either Chesterton or Belloc, or any serious Catholic, would endorse getting drunk. But these two men, with their pipes and pints and songs about the Cross, show that Catholicism is not dead or tiresome, in spite of what its cultured despisers may accuse. Catholicism is emphatically alive and unquestionably jovial. It's a home for partiers and anyone who agrees that life is worth celebrating.

THE ORDINARY MAN

Speaking of Chesterton, it was an umbrella that played a key role in him becoming Catholic. The English convert said that whenever he went to non-Catholic churches, he would usually leave his umbrella by the back door during the worship service. In these churches, as expected, his umbrella would always be there afterward. But the first time he went into a Catholic parish to hear Mass, he was stunned to find that his umbrella had disappeared after the service—someone had stolen it. Surprisingly, Chesterton wasn't angry; he smiled. Though he was upset at losing his umbrella, he was happy to discover a new fact: the Catholic Church really was for everyone. Chesterton, the self-confessed sinner, came to believe that if the Catholic Church offered such a generous and open doorway to the rabble and the shufflers, both sinners and saints, then he had indeed found a home where he could also fumble his way into heaven.[54]

The same fact struck Dorothy Day, a famous New Yorker convert to Catholicism. As she visited churches and spotted the poor and outcast praying alongside the elite, she felt *this* was the religion for her. It was the only faith she found that displayed the full spectrum of human diversity. It welcomed not just the rich and powerful but also the poor and ordinary.

For confirmation, just scan through a list of the Church's saints. While it does contain many influential rulers, you'll find many men and women who were surprisingly ordinary. You'll meet painters, carpenters, doorkeepers, and stay-at-home moms. You'll discover people who were homeless, out of a job, or plagued by family tensions. In other words, you'll find *ordinary* people, like you and me.

The Catholic Church has long championed the common humans, standing for their rights and elevating their dignity. It agrees with Chesterton that "the most extraordinary thing in the world is an ordinary man, his ordinary wife, and their ordinary family."

As an ordinary man myself, I'm delighted that Catholicism doesn't have stiff membership requirements. It doesn't require members to have special talents or positions of honor. You don't need impressive spiritual credentials. The Catholic Church welcomes—even celebrates—the most ordinary among us, even as the rest of the world passes us by.

THE SKEPTIC

People sometimes think that to be religious in general, or Catholic in particular, you can't have any doubts or struggles. You must have an unwavering confidence in all your religious beliefs and never a weak moment.

But this simply isn't true. Catholicism is a welcome home for doubters. This doesn't mean doubt in itself is a good thing. Of course, given the choice, we would all prefer to be sure of our beliefs than doubt them.

But while the Catholic Church teaches many dogmas that are basic and required for all believers, such as the existence of God, the divinity of Jesus, and the wrongness of murdering innocent people, the Church is sensitive to the fact that all believers struggle, at one time or another, with their beliefs. Even saints such as Mother Teresa, St. John of the Cross, and St. Thérèse of Lisieux went through dark periods of spiritual confusion and despair. So if you're not 100 percent clear and confident in your beliefs, you're in very good company.

It's important to note that beyond the Church's core beliefs, there's a pretty wide umbrella. In other words, the Church doesn't delineate exactly what you should believe about every issue under the sun. When it comes to scientific or political questions, for example, the Church provides broad principles but leaves it up to individual Catholics to wrestle with the specifics.

It also understands that most of us waffle back and forth in terms of confidence. For instance, on some days you might believe God exists, but on other days the evil in the world overwhelms you and causes you to doubt. Part of you thinks Jesus might really have risen from the dead, but then another part says that's just so wild and miraculous and the evidence is too buried in history.

Wherever you're at, Catholicism is a welcome place for skeptics. That's because it's one of the rare faiths that actually takes skepticism seriously, treating doubters with respect and sensitivity, and refusing to dismiss their concerns. It's not afraid of difficult questions (again, see Aquinas's *Summa* for proof of this). Instead, it's open to engaging them. The Church rejects trite, simplistic answers to important questions, refusing to shut down dialogue out of fear that its teachings may be proven wrong.

THE SINNER

It's maybe the most startling part of the Church's beautiful diversity: its emphatic love for sinners. Most self-aware people know they fall way short of the Church's moral demands and could never come close to meeting them, at least not any time soon. So why bother?

Unfortunately, this despair is often compounded by hurtful comments or bad experiences, where supposedly loving Catholics have demeaned them, judged them, or failed to welcome them with sensitivity and grace.

But what's sad is that the conclusion gets things exactly backward. To put it simply, the Church exists for sinners. The Church is not a museum for saints but a hospital for the spiritually sick. Jesus reiterates this over and over in the Gospels, dismissing the healthy and self-justified and instead focusing on those who knew they needed healing. Pope John Paul II, a pope few would accuse of being lax on morality, picked up on the same idea by proposing the "law of gradualism," which suggests that even though the Church's moral standards are unchanging—since they were given by God, or through God's Church, and thus we can't tamper with them—we can recognize that most people gradually come to meet these standards. Few of us have experienced an instant and complete moral conversion. For example, talk candidly with anyone who has been addicted to pornography and they'll confirm its powerful grip. It often takes years before someone recognizes the damage that porn has inflicted on his mind, his relationships, and his faith and finally decides to cut it out. But as with many addictions, he may get sucked back in after a few days of abstaining. This cycle repeats itself over and over—two steps forward and one step back, several days of success interspersed with moments of moral failure.

So how does the Catholic Church respond to someone such as that, someone who is struggling against sin, trying to become a better person, but nevertheless falls again and again? The answer is, with grace. Some in that situation may think, Ah, there's no place for me in the Catholic Church. I will always be grappling with [insert sin here]. The Church doesn't want a failure like me. However, just the opposite is true. The Church exists for moral failures. It isn't for the perfect but for the struggling, those who want to be healed and are looking for a divine healer.

Every saint has a past, every sinner has a future. Perhaps the most beautiful thing about the Church is that it not only houses the homeless but also refuses to send sinners away.

CONCLUSION

Join the Rebellion

As a vaguely religious college student, about to graduate as an engineer, I was probably one of the last people you'd expect to become Catholic.

But I did. I chose it for myself. Nobody forced or enticed me. In fact, many people questioned the decision.

But I knew I had to enter the Church because after a long period of study, and much discussion and reflection, I saw in Catholicism the fullness of truth, goodness, and beauty—not just small, fleeting instances of each but the fullest expressions I had ever encountered, even their very origins. My heart starved for these transcendentals, and it was the Church that finally fed it.

I of course knew the Catholic Church seemed strange and backward to the world, and this disturbed me, but only until I discovered it was the world that had turned itself around. The Church was the still point; the culture was in orbit. And to a wobbling culture, everything seemed off course.

But still, I was nervous about becoming Catholic. What would it mean for my relationships? How would my family react? How would it change my day-to-day life?

You might be asking the same questions. Even if you're compelled by the arguments in this book, you're probably still on the fence. You may have a new appreciation for the Catholic Church, but you're not quite ready for the huge next step of actually becoming Catholic. That's alright. As with any major life decision, it's not one to take lightly or rush into. But to continue your exploration, here are some great suggestions that really helped me over the fence.

READ OTHER STORIES

During my conversion, stories of other Catholic converts proved a big help. One of the best sources is the website WhyImCatholic.com. There you'll find dozens of stories, nicely arranged by religious background. For instance, you'll find entries from former atheists, Jews, Evangelical Protestants, Muslims, and Buddhists—even a group of self-described pagan witches! These stories will provide two things for you: they'll confirm the questions and doubts you likely have, showing you that you're not the only one who has them, but they'll also highlight the best ways to think through them.

You can also find several great conversion stories in print. Here are some of my favorites:

- *Apologia Pro Vita Sua*, by John Henry Newman (a former Anglican)

- *Confessions*, by St. Augustine (a former pagan)
- *From Willow Creek to Sacred Heart: Rekindling My Love for Catholicism*, by Chris Haw (a former Evangelical Protestant)
- *The Long Loneliness*, by Dorothy Day (a former Communist "none")
- *Night's Bright Darkness: A Modern Conversion Story*, by Sally Read (a former atheist)
- *Not God's Type: An Atheist Academic Lays Down Her Arms*, by Holly Ordway (a former atheist)
- *Rome Sweet Home: Our Journey to Catholicism*, by Scott Hahn (a former Presbyterian Protestant) and Kimberly Hahn
- *Salvation Is from the Jews: The Role of Judaism in Salvation History from Abraham to the Second Coming*, by Roy H. Schoeman (a former Jew)
- *Seven Storey Mountain*, by Thomas Merton (a former bohemian "none")
- *Something Other Than God: How I Passionately Sought Happiness and Accidentally Found It*, by Jennifer Fulwiler (a former atheist)
- *Surprised by Truth: 11 Converts Give the Biblical and Historical Reasons for Becoming Catholic*, edited by Patrick Madrid (multiple backgrounds)
- *Why I Am a Catholic*, by G. K. Chesterton (a former agnostic)

GET ANSWERS TO YOUR QUESTIONS

After reading some conversion stories, you'll next want to address any particular objections you have to Catholicism. There's virtually no objection or challenge the Church *hasn't* seen (and answered) over the past two thousand years. So take heart and know you're not the first to propose it.

Answers to such objections are widely available. You might first start with the website Catholic.com, run by the Catholic Answers apostolate, which exists to explain and defend the Catholic faith. They have hundreds of articles, videos, tracts, books, and podcasts available through their website. Your best friend there is the "search" box at the top. Just type in any topic or question, and you'll find customized answers to help you out. Catholic Answers even keeps track of the most-searched terms to ensure they have plenty of resources on those topics. (Their most-searched term is *purgatory*.)

Another great resource is a website I founded called *StrangeNotions.com*. It's the central place of dialogue between Catholics and atheists, features more than thirty expert contributors (scientists, philosophers, theologians, artists, and more), and is the perfect place if you're curious about life's Big Questions. If you're wondering whether God exists, how we engage moral questions, or about the relationships between science and faith, you'll find lots of helpful resources. If you're coming from an atheist or agnostic background, make this your first stop.

Finally, the work of Bishop Robert Barron was pivotal in my own conversion. He's perhaps the smartest and most eloquent explainer of the Catholic faith today (and I don't just say that because I work for him!). His epic ten-part *Catholicism* film series, which aired on PBS and was seen by millions of people, offers a beautiful, sweeping look at the Church, and his many resources at WordOnFire.org are designed to answer the most pressing questions and challenges you may have. As you explore Catholicism, bookmark that site and check it often.

THE NEXT STEPS

But what happens then? You've read and studied. You've considered the case for Catholicism. And now you're convinced: you want to become Catholic. First, congratulations on deciding to join the only serious rebellion left. But second, you'll need to take a few final steps.

Connect with a Parish

The first thing you should do is contact a local Catholic parish. Find a list of nearby Catholic parishes by visiting MassTimes.org. Just enter your city, state, or zip (or use GPS on your phone), and it will show the nearest Catholic churches. Check out their websites, find one that seems vibrant and welcoming, and then call or e-mail the parish to ask what you should do if you're interested in becoming Catholic.

But a word of warning: it's possible that the first person you encounter at the parish—a receptionist, an usher, a director of religious education, and so on—will be less than welcoming. This isn't to say all parishes are unreceptive to people exploring the Catholic faith, just that many are short-handed and run by weary volunteers. Many parishes have teens answering their phones, and while these young people often have a lot of enthusiasm, energy, and good intentions, they might not have developed a lot of judgment and discretion. To be frank, they might have no clue how to handle someone such as you who is seriously interested in becoming Catholic. So brace yourself for the possibility that some people won't be helpful or understanding. Just remember: you're becoming Catholic because you're convinced Catholicism is true, good, and beautiful, not because the Church is full of perfectly nice people. Be patient with them, or if you'd rather, just move on and try another parish. That's okay too.

Talk with a Priest

Once you choose a good parish, the next step is to connect with a priest there. This is probably the most important step. A priest will be able to talk with you, assess your situation, and determine the best next steps. This doesn't mean you have to sit down face-to-face with him, if that makes you a little nervous (it's normal to feel that way). Many of my non-religious friends clam up around priests—or really around *any* religious figures. Instead, see if you can get the priest's e-mail address from the church office and send him a brief message. Tell him you've been reading and exploring, and you're interested in becoming Catholic. However you do it, connecting with a priest will prove very helpful.

Join RCIA at a Local Parish

Chances are high that if you've never been Catholic, or if you've been away from the Church for many years, you'll probably be asked to enroll in RCIA (Rite of Christian Initiation of Adults). RCIA is a free course for prospective converts or reverts, hosted at every Catholic parish. Groups usually meet weekly, and the meetings typically include a talk on a particular Catholic topic with time for discussion and personal reflection. It's a great way to get up to speed on all the details about the Catholic faith. It's also the perfect place to ask questions, discuss doubts, or clear up confusions. Each parish has a designated RCIA instructor. Classes usually begin in the fall and end with full initiation during the Easter Vigil (i.e., the Saturday night Mass before Easter Sunday). And just to be clear: signing up for RCIA *does not* mean you've already decided to be Catholic. It's an exploratory group. Many people sign up and then drop out because they're just not ready. So don't feel that by signing up for RCIA you're committing to something more—you're not.

One note from experience: don't be disheartened if, due to timing, you have to go through several months of RCIA before entering the Catholic Church. When I was in college and became convinced that Catholicism was true, I wanted to become Catholic immediately. Why wait? I thought. But I was deflated upon discovering that I had to participate in six months of RCIA classes first. However, that ended up being a wonderful period, a time of significant learning and growth in my life. So however long the wait, don't give up. The end will be well worth the journey.

Go Deeper in Your Faith

Finally, one of the biggest mistake new Catholics make is thinking that the conversion process stops when they become Catholic. This is why a regretfully high number of converts end up drifting back away from the Church. Don't make that mistake! Choosing to become Catholic is like entering through a doorway into a vast room filled with endlessly fascinating treasures. One lifetime is not nearly enough to explore it all (which is one reason God gives us eternal life!). After you become Catholic, tap into these resources. Join a Bible study or a faith-sharing group at the parish. Start reading Catholic websites. Find good Catholic books, and build a solid home library (a great part about being Catholic is that the majority of our spiritual classics are centuries old and thus in the public domain, which means you can get them for pennies). However you choose to do it, decide that once you become Catholic, it's the first step—not the last—down a much deeper and exciting journey.

There are many good reasons to become Catholic. But as we've seen in this book, the best reason is because the paths of truth, goodness, and beauty all converge at the door of the Catholic Church.

I walked those paths, and opened that door, eight years ago. It was the best decision I've ever made. Inside I found unmistakable wisdom, fascinating people, breathtaking spiritual experiences, and missing keys to life that I had been hunting for years, keys that opened up so many mysteries from love to morality and meaning. Most importantly I found God, and I encountered him more deeply and profoundly than ever before.

I'm not the only one who has made those discoveries. Every year, millions of people walk the same path. They enter the Catholic Church from different places and backgrounds. Some journeys are smooth; others, more difficult. Yet they all come searching for the same things—truth, goodness, and beauty—and when they push open the door of the Church, they find them in sparkling profusion.

Today, that same door remains waiting for you, and it remains unlocked. You only need to come and knock.

If your heart hungers for something more than what you've found elsewhere, I beckon you to try that door and discover all that waits on the other side.

APPENDIX

Going Deeper

During my conversion to Catholicism, I read scores of books from a wide range of genres—history, theology, philosophy, science, biography, and memoir—that helped me see the Catholic Church from different angles. I've since read hundreds more. Most books proved good, but some were excellent. Here are the ten that have best helped clarify the case for Catholicism:

- *Answering Atheism: How to Make the Case for God with Logic and Charity*, by Trent Horn

- *Catholic Christianity: A Complete Catechism of Catholic Church Beliefs Based on the Catechism of the Catholic Church*, by Peter Kreeft

- *The Catholic Church and Conversion*, by G. K. Chesterton

- *Catholicism: A Journey to the Heart of the Faith*, by Robert Barron

- *The Four Witnesses: The Early Church in Her Own Words*, by Rod Bennett

- *Fundamentals of the Faith: Essays in Christian Apologetics*, by Peter Kreeft
- *The Lamb's Supper: The Mass as Heaven on Earth*, by Scott Hahn
- *Rome Sweet Home: Our Journey to Catholicism*, by Scott and Kimberly Hahn
- *Theology for Beginners*, by Frank J. Sheed
- *To Know Christ Jesus*, by Frank J. Sheed

Notes

1. G. K. Chesterton, "Why I Am a Catholic," from *Twelve Modern Apostles and Their Creeds* (1926), reprinted in *The Collected Works of G. K. Chesterton*, vol. 3 (San Francisco: Ignatius Press, 1990).

2. As quoted in Wesley C. Salmon, "Religion and Science: A New Look at Hume's Dialogues," *Philosophical Studies 33*, no. 2 (1978): 176.

3. See Peter Kreeft, "20 Arguments for God's Existence," Strange Notions, accessed January 28, 2017, http://www.strangenotions.com/god-exists.

4. Thanks to William Lane Craig for this example.

5. Alexander Vilenkin, cited in Lisa Grossman, "Why Physicists Can't Avoid a Creation Event," *New Scientist*, January 11, 2012.

6. Alexander Vilenkin, *Many Worlds in One: The Search for Other Universes* (New York: Hill and Wang, 2006), 176.

7. "America's Changing Religious Landscape," Pew Research Center, May 12, 2015, 3, http://www.pewforum.org/2015/05/12/americas-changing-religious-landscape.

8. Ibid., 12.

9. See San Diego State University, "Millennials: The Least Religious Generation," ScienceDaily, May 27, 2015, https://www.sciencedaily.com/releases/2015/05/150527124727.htm.

10. Thanks to Bishop Robert Barron for pointing out this Newman insight. See John Henry Newman, *Difficulties of Anglicans*, vol. 2 (London, 1891), 80–81.

11. Quoted by Nick Spencer, "Is Religion Good for You? Analysing Three Decades Worth of Academic Research on the Relationship between Religion and Well-Being," *Religion and the Public Sphere* (blog), June 28, 2016, http://blogs.lse.ac.uk/religionpublicsphere/2016/06/

is-religion-good-for-you-analysing-three-decades-worth-of-academic-research-on-the-relationship-between-religion-and-well-being.

12. Pew Research Center, "2014 U.S. Religious Landscape Study," conducted June 4–September 30, 2014. http://www.pewforum.org/religious-landscape-study.

13. C. S. Lewis, "What Are We to Make of Jesus Christ?" (1950), in *The Essential C. S. Lewis*, ed. Lyle W. Dorsett (New York: Touchstone, 1996), 330–33.

14. I'm indebted here to the work of William Lane Craig. See especially William Lane Craig, *Reasonable Faith: Christian Truth and Apologetics*, 3rd ed. (Wheaton, IL: Crossway Books, 2008).

15. For a full defense of this "minimal facts" argument for the Resurrection, see the work of Gary R. Habermas, especially the magisterial book he cowrote with Michael R. Licona, titled *The Case for the Resurrection of Jesus* (Grand Rapids, MI: Kregel Publications, 2004).

16. See Habermas and Licona, *The Case for the Resurrection*. See also Michael R. Licona, *The Resurrection of Jesus: A New Historiographical Approach* (Downers Grove, IL: IVP Academic, 2010). Licona writes, "These scholars span a very wide range of theological and philosophical convictions and include atheists, agnostics, Jews and Christians who make their abode at both ends of the theological spectrum and everywhere in between. We therefore have the heterogeneity we desire in a consensus, and this gives us confidence that our horizons will not lead us completely astray" (280).

17. G. K. Chesterton, *The Autobiography of G. K. Chesterton* (San Francisco: Ignatius Press, 2006), 217.

18. Paul VI, *Declaration on the Relation of the Church to Non-Christian Religions* (*Nostra Aetate*), sec. 2, October 28, 1965, http://www.vatican.va/archive/hist_councils/ii_vatican_council/documents/vat-ii_decl_19651028_nostra-aetate_en.html.

19. G. K. Chesterton, *Alarms and Discursions* (London: Methuen, 1910).

20. Hilaire Belloc, *Survivals and New Arrivals* (Rockford, IL: Tan Books and Publishers, 1992, originally 1929), 165.

21. Thomas E. Woods Jr., "Commentary: History Shows Contributions of Catholic Church to Western Civilization," *Deseret News*, December 28, 2011, http://www.deseretnews.com/article/700210479/

Commentary-History-shows-contributions-of-Catholic-Church-to-Western-civilization.html.

22. Quoted in Robert Barron, "The Myth of the War between Science and Religion," Word on Fire, December 8, 2008, https://www.word onfire.org/resources/article/the-myth-of-the-war-between-science-and-religion/331.

23. Thomas E. Wood Jr., *How the Catholic Church Built Western Civilization* (Washington, DC: Regency, 2005), 4.

24. Ibid.

25. Originally in Duncan Aikman, *New York Times Magazine*, February 1933, quoted in Simon Singh, "Even Einstein Had His Off Days," *New York Times*, January 2, 2005.

26. See Stacy Trasancos, *Science Was Born of Christianity: The Teaching of Fr. Stanley L. Jaki* (Orlando, FL: Habitation of Chimham Publishing, 2014).

27. Once again, thanks to Bishop Robert Barron for these insights.

28. Woods, "Commentary."

29. Quoted in Charles Paulino, "A Missionary Unafraid to Live and Die with His People," *L'Osservatore Romano* (English edition), October 14, 2009.

30. Ibid.

31. Ibid.

32. Quoted by Missionaries of Charity, Archdiocese of New York, http://catholiccharitiesny.org/our-agencies/missionaries-charity.

33. Teresa of Calcutta, *One Heart Full of Love*, ed. Jose Luis Gonzales-Balado (Cincinnati: Servant Books, 1988), 7.

34. John Henry Newman, *Development of Christian Doctrine*, 1.7.

35. Chesterton, "Why I Am a Catholic," 110.

36. Fulton Sheen, foreword to *Radio Replies*, vol. 1 by Leslie Rumble and Charles M. Carty (St. Paul, MN: Radio Replies Press, 1938), ix.

37. Sarah, "Christian Formation and the Cost of the Culture Wars," *A Queer Calling* (blog), May 1, 2014, http://aqueercalling.com/2014/05/01/christian-formation-and-the-cost-of-the-culture-wars.

38. Austen Ivereigh and Kathryn Jean Lopez, *How to Defend the Faith without Raising Your Voice: Civil Responses to Catholic Hot-Button Issues*, rev. and updated ed. (Huntington, IN: Our Sunday Visitor, 2015), 188.

39. Chesterton, "Why I Am a Catholic," 127.

40. G. K. Chesterton, "Christmas Thoughts on Vivisection," *The Illustrated London News*, January 4, 1908, quoted in *The Collected Works of G. K. Chesterton: The Illustrated London News, 1908–1910* (San Francisco: Ignatius Press, 1987), 17.

41. Thanks to Bishop Robert Barron for this language.

42. Woods, *How the Catholic Church Built Western Civilization*, 119.

43. Paul Johnson, *Art: A New History* (New York: HarperCollins, 2003), 153.

44. Pontifical Council for Culture, *The Via Pulchritudinis: Privileged Pathway for Evangelisation and Dialogue* (2006), III.2.

45. Will Durant, *The Renaissance*, vol. 5 of *The Story of Civilization* (New York: MJF Books, 1953), 484.

46. See Woods, *How the Catholic Church Built Western Civilization*, 132.

47. See Peter J. Kreeft and Ronald K. Tacelli, *Handbook of Catholic Apologetics: Reasoned Answers to Questions of Faith* (San Francisco: Ignatius Press, 2009).

48. Quoted in Karl Keating, "What Was Lost Is Found: Paul Claudel Returns to Me," *Catholic Answers* (blog), January 30, 2013, https://www.catholic.com/magazine/online-edition/what-was-lost-is-found-paul-claudel-returns-to-me.

49. Ibid.

50. Ibid.

51. See Plato, *The Symposium*, 210–12.

52. Paul Camacho, "A Conversation with Peter Kreeft," *Boston College Observer*, April 22, 2004.

53. Robert Barron, "You're Holier Than You Know," *U.S. Catholic*, July 1, 2008.

54. Thanks to Dr. Tom Neal for highlighting this story for me.

Brandon Vogt is a bestselling and award-winning author, blogger, and speaker who serves as content director for Bishop Robert Barron's Word on Fire Catholic Ministries.

Vogt was one of the millennial "nones" when it came to religion until, as a mechanical engineering student at Florida State University, he began a passionate search for truth. That search led him unexpectedly to the Catholic Church in 2008. In 2013, he started *StrangeNotions.com*, the largest site of dialogue between Catholics and atheists.

Vogt was named one of the "Top 30 Catholics under 30" by FOCUS as well as one of the "Top 30 Catholics to Follow on Twitter." He is the author of seven books, including *RETURN: How to Draw Your Child Back to the Church* and *The Church and New Media. Why I Am Catholic (and You Should Be Too)* won first place in the 2018 Catholic Press Association book awards for popular presentation of the faith. His work has been featured by media outlets including NPR, Fox News, CBS, EWTN, *America* magazine, Vatican Radio, *Our Sunday Visitor*, *National Review*, and *Christianity Today*. He is a regular guest on Catholic radio and speaks to a variety of audiences about evangelization, new media, Catholic social teaching, and spirituality.

www.brandonvogt.com
www.claritasu.com
strangenotions.com

AVE
AVE MARIA PRESS

Founded in 1865, Ave Maria Press,
a ministry of the Congregation of
Holy Cross, is a Catholic publishing
company that serves the spiritual and
formative needs of the Church and its
schools, institutions, and ministers;
Christian individuals and families; and
others seeking spiritual nourishment.

For a complete listing of titles from

Ave Maria Press

Sorin Books

Forest of Peace

Christian Classics

visit www.avemariapress.com

AVE MARIA PRESS
AVE Notre Dame, IN
A Ministry of the United States Province of Holy Cross